the new work by
Arthur Miller

the Misfits

KING

In an early scene, Gaylord tells Roslyn a joke about a city man asking a country bumpkin for directions to a town. The bumpkin can't help him. Lostness is a running motif in the film. So is lack of knowledge. When Perce asks Roslyn if she belongs to Gay, she replies, "I don't know where I belong." When Guido runs into trouble in his airplane he says, "I can't make a landing and I can't get up to God." Whether the characters are in bars or trucks or roaming around the desert, they have a sense of aimlessness. They both embrace and fear this.

Guido inhabits an unfinished house. The clocks in Isabelle's house are stopped. Perce has been evicted from his family home. Gay and Roslyn fall into one another's arms from a shared rootlessness. "I always end up back where I started," Roslyn complains. Isabelle has a broken arm.

Isabelle's stopped clocks echo Charles Dickens' Miss Havisham in portraying a world where life stalled after romance died in *Great Expectations*. Her broken arm, like Roslyn's dented Cadillac and Perce's ravaged face, present us with a world where things fall apart. The center cannot hold. Guido's battered plane and his overgrown garden also tap into this sense of damage.

Miller sometimes over-eggs the omelette of brokenness. Early on we get the message that it's a symbol of psychological pain. He drives the message home in too many of the scenes for comfort. It's one of the weaknesses of the film.

Another one is the romance between Gaylord and Roslyn. We don't see him becoming passionate about her at any point. Boiled down to essentials, their relationship doesn't really go much further than the affection she shares with Perce. Would this be enough for a man of Gay's years to throw up everything he'd spent his life doing to be with her? It's doubtful.

The screenplay was less propagandist than some of Miller's earlier work but there's still contrivance in many of the lines. This is notwithstanding their folksiness. He hides his high-sounding ideas about love and life behind an "aw shucks" phraseology.

As well as being broken, the characters suffer from a variety of thwarted ambitions. Guido wanted to become a doctor. Perce failed in his dream of becoming a rodeo rider. Gay's marriage collapsed.

Roslyn's dreams of being a dancer died. Guido lost a wife and baby in childbirth. Perce lost his father in a hunting accident. Gay was betrayed by his wife. Roslyn was divorced by a husband who went on to marry her best friend.

*The Misfits* signals both endings and beginnings. If it was the "last" western, as is sometimes claimed, it also ushered in a new decade, the decade of hope and liberation, the decade of John F. Kennedy.

Competition from television made directors like Huston push the envelope. He was heartened by European influence. So was Miller. The film industry was opening up. There was room for disenchantment, for the offbeat, for nuance.

It wasn't a Clark Gable film. It wasn't a Marilyn Monroe film. It wasn't a Montgomery Clift one or a John Huston one either. It was an Arthur Miller film.

According to one writer, Miller tried to do for the cowboys in the film what Hemingway had tried to do for bullfighters in his stories: blow away the smokescreens and locate the real people underneath.[2]

Miller based his story on experience. He was in Reno in 1956 to establish the six week residency necessary to procure a divorce from his first wife, Mary Slattery, so he could marry Monroe.

He rented a shack at Pyramid Lake, fifty miles northeast of Reno. He became friends with the woman living next door to him, a divorcee called Peggy Marsh. One day she asked him to accompany her to the house of a woman she knew in Quail Canyon, a Mrs. Stix. Miller went with her in her car. It was there that he met the cowboys he featured in his story. They were heading off to rope some horses at the time so they could sell them for pet food.

Miller accompanied them on a trip to the mountains where they chased some mustangs towards a lake, lassoing them from a moving truck. The ropes were tied to tires they dropped from their trucks, the weight making it impossible for the horses to keep running.

The men were heavy drinkers. He saw them as confirmed bachelors with an exaggerated sense of their lady-killer potential. They were throwbacks to a vanishing frontier in his eyes.[3]

At his request they told him how they came to do what they did. Before World War II, they said, the mountains were full of mustangs. There was a good market for them as children's ponies. But then things changed. After the war ended, children turned their attention to more mechanical items. They preferred motorbikes to horses as a mode of transport. The result was that horses were now sold to be slaughtered. It was the mustanger's job to catch them. He first tried to isolate them for their herd. This was often done from the air. His associates followed the stray horses by truck, roping them as they fled to lakes for water. They received six cents a pound for the meat.

They brought Miller to a house they stayed in sometimes. It was an abandoned shack in the middle of nowhere. They slept in it when they had nowhere else to go. One of the windows was broken. A door hung on a single hinge. There were western novels and copies of *Playboy* magazine on the floor. The men dreamed of playing cowboys in films. The movie cowboy was the real one, they thought. They were the imitations.[4]

He wrote the story when Monroe was filming *The Prince and the Showgirl*. He submitted it to a number of magazines that rejected it because of its length. It was finally accepted by *Esquire* in a slightly truncated form. He expanded the role of Roslyn not only to fulfill Monroe but also to kick start his screenwriting career. It filled the gap left by the writer's block he was going through at the time as regards playwrighting.

It sounded like a good idea in theory, a project to advance the careers both of an actress who wanted to be taken seriously and an author who was anxious to develop a new direction for himself. Unfortunately it turned into a disaster. Both cast and crew watched their relationship unravelling in fast motion in front of them.

It's impossible to look at the film today without seeing it as the swan song of two if not three of its lead players. Such a purview covers it with layers of tragedy already endemic in the script but amplified by what would happen to such a triumvirate afterwards.

There was a huge publicity drive around the film. Over fifteen location reports were written every day for the syndicates, with other reports being phoned to them from Los Angeles and New York.

Tensions were manifest from the outset. It wasn't only Monroe's marriage that was crumbling; it was the woman herself. Her pill intake increased on the set, as did her alcohol consumption and her burgeoning depression. The farther she drifted away from Miller the more she came closer to her acting coach, Paula Strasberg. Strasberg threatened to derail the production on more than one occasion as a result of his inordinate influence on Monroe. The cast and crew were swiftly delineated into two camps. Monroe headed one of them; Miller the other.

If Miller wasn't the screenwriter of the film, or at least such an active one as he proved to be, the pair's problems could have been handled delicately and become a sidebar to the shooting of it. Sadly, that was never going to be the case. It was a film that was conceived jointly and it played itself out in the same way. Both of them would have needed to give Oscar-winning performances to conceal their alienation from one another.

For Gable, the title of the film summed it up: "Miller, Monroe and Clift - they don't know what the hell they're doing."[5] Its French translation was "Les Desaxes" - "The Unbalanced." Maybe this was more appropriate.

*The Misfits*, as Axel Madsen pointed out, casts a long shadow: "By the time of its release, Clark Gable was dead and Marilyn Monroe

and Arthur Miller had broken up. A year and a half later, Monroe committed suicide. Five years later Montgomery Clift was dead."[6]

The circumstances of the night Monroe died have exercised the imagination of more amateur screenwriters than one can shake a stick at. Everyone from Jimmy Hoffa to Sam Giancana has somehow been implicated in a psycho-drama that has all the melodrama of a fifth-rate thriller Monroe might have made at the beginning of her career.

Where were all the conspiracy theories coming from? Yes she knew some people in powerful places but she wasn't Mata Hari. She was a film start who had a tryst with a politician, end of story. And even that wasn't fully proven.

*The Misfits* is often shown on late night TV channels in the decades since it was made. It's also a favourite at film festivals and has attained cult status at some of these. In the present book I attempt to explain why.

# Background

Marilyn Monroe decided to put on her business hat in 1954 after finishing *The Seven Year Itch*. She set up Marilyn Monroe Productions with her friend Milton Greene to give her more control over her career. Not everyone was convinced she had "the smarts" to make anything of that. She was satirized in *Will Success Spoil Rock Hunter?* Frank Tashlin's satire of a dumb blonde who does something similar. "I carry Marilyn Monroe around with me like an albatross," she said once.[1]

She left Hollywood for New York and started attending classes at the Actors Studio. She also took private lessons at the house of Joe Strasberg, who presided over the classes. She became friendly with his wife Paula and daughter Susan. Paula would soon replace Natasha Lytess as her acting coach.

She was now dating Arthur Miller. She'd met him briefly in 1951. At that time she was grieving over the death of Johnny Hyde, the man who more than anything else had launched her film career without seeking anything in return. Miller was touched that she should be so emotional.[2]

Miller was eleven years older than her. She had a preference for older men. Joe DiMaggio, her former husband, was older than her too. Yves Montand, with whom she would have an affair during her marriage to Miller, was five years older than her. She didn't sleep with Hyde but she enjoyed his company. He was old enough to be her father. So was Joe Schenck, a movie mogul whom she slept with. Monroe adopted a childlike persona in many of her films. This fed into the perception that she spent most of her life searching for a father figure. Her orphaned upbringing meant that she was denied one in her youth.

In a conversation with Shelley Winters once, she listed the following among her list of ideal lovers: Ernest Hemingway, Charles Laughton, Clifford Odets and Albert Einstein. These too were

*Arthur Miller proudly leads his wife around Reno.*

all significantly older than her, especially Einstein.³ Her heart belonged to Daddy.

The relationship with Miller moved fast. It wasn't long before they became engaged to be married. Monroe was about to make a film in London, *The Prince and the Showgirl*. Miller's play *A View from the Bridge* had recently been a hit on Broadway and was soon to have a London showing so he had a reason to go to England with her.

Their forthcoming wedding captured as many headlines as that of Grace Kelly and Prince Rainier, or "Prince Reindeer" as Monroe called him, but the day itself was blighted by tragedy. Shortly before the wedding ceremony, a journalist called Mara Scherbatoff - she was actually a princess - was following the Miller vehicle to their Roxbury farm in a car driven by the brother of her photographer. Miller's cousin Morton was driving Miller and Monroe. He knew the twists and turns in the road since he lived on it but Scherbatoff's driver didn't. That was his downfall.

Scherbatoff's car skidded out of control at a bad bend near Miller's house and crashed into a tree. Miller saw the crash through his rear view mirror. He pulled up and ran back to survey the damage. He told Monroe not to follow him but she did. They were both traumatized when they saw the extent of Scherbatoff's injuries. She'd been thrown through the windshield. Inside the car her driver was seriously injured as well.

Miller called for an ambulance. When he was informed there would be a two hour delay before it arrived he said, "I think you should know that it's Marilyn Monroe back there on the road and this story is going to be on the front pages of every newspaper in the world tomorrow." His fib produced the desired result. An ambulance was dispatched immediately. But it was in vain, Sherbatoff's injuries were too severe for anything to be done for her.[4]

As Monroe bent over the dying woman her sweater became stained with blood. When she went back to Morton's house to change, photographers swarmed around her. One of them fell from a tree.[5] Scherbatoff died in hospital a few hours later. Both of them saw it as a bad omen for their marriage.

The last thing Miller and Monroe wanted at this point was to have to face the press and feign good humor. They answered questions monosyllabically without mentioning the crash. They stood under a tree like the one that had been responsible for Scherbatoff's death. Such an irony must have intensified their grief. They were married that evening in a civil ceremony that lasted less than five minutes. They had a Jewish one two days later. Monroe's conversion to Judaism led to her films being banned in Egypt.

Their union was variously described in the press as the alliance between an owl and a pussycat or an egghead and an hourglass. Such clichés ignored the fact that, when they married, Monroe was going through a period of trying to downplay her sex bomb status and Miller was seeking to outgrow his "absent-minded professor" image.

For Monroe this was easier said than done, even after she set up Marilyn Monroe Productions. Ann Baxter, her co-star in *All About Eve*, once said of her, "She was smart for only ten minutes of her entire life. That was the time it took her to sign with Twentieth Century-Fox.[6]

The trip to London meant Miller had to apply for a passport. It brought him to the attention of the House Un-American Activities Committee (HUAC). HUAC had denied him a passport in 1954 because of his perceived link with communist writers. He was asked what the purpose of his trip was before he married Monroe. He replied, simply, "I wish to attend a production of my play and to be with the woman who will then be my wife."[7]

The passport was granted and two weeks after they were married they left for London. Monroe's co-star in *The Prince and the Showgirl* was Laurence Olivier. He was also directing the film. He was married to Vivien Leigh at the time. Monroe didn't get on with Leigh. "She didn't like me," she said. "She thought I stole her part."[8] Leigh had played the role in the stage version.

Leigh was worried that Monroe would have an affair with her husband but she didn't have any cause to be concerned. Monroe and Olivier didn't like one another. He was too stiff for her and she was too giggly for him. At times they seemed to be making a different film. There was also a certain amount of power play going on. Any thoughts Olivier might have had that she would genuflect before him were rapidly erased. She saw him as too theatrical. He patronized her in a manner that might have intimidated her as a younger woman. There was no danger of that now. She saw herself on an equal footing with him.

Miller found himself at a loose end in London. He vetted some film scripts that had been sent to Monroe and compiled press clippings for her. At times he felt like her flunky. He started writing *The Misfits* but other than that he was idle. His role was more that being "Mr. Monroe" than hers of "Mrs. Miller." She complained about Olivier to him frequently.

Part of Olivier's problems with Monroe concerned her legendary unpunctuality. One day his patience gave out and he said to her, "Why can't you get here on time, for fuck's sake?" Quick as a beat she shot back, "Oh. Do you have that word in England too?"[9]

Anecdotes about Olivier bullying her on the set of *The Prince and the Showgirl* should be seen in the light of the executive hat she wore in this film. It was released through her production company so Olivier was in effect her employee. The prince was working for the showgirl.

Olivier said "Be sexy" to her during one scene. As if she could be anything else! Paula Strasberg had different advice. "Think of Frank Sinatra and Coca Cola," she advised. Maybe Olivier would have preferred Caruso and champagne.

*A rare group shot of the cast.*

"Be sexy." That was like asking snow to be white. But strangely she couldn't. Olivier was too formal to bring out that side of her. She may also have bridled at the insinuation that it was the only quality she represented for him. The upshot of the comment was to increase the tension that had already been simmering between the two.

After two frustrating weeks on the set of the film, Miller flew back to New York to see his children. Monroe suffered a miscarriage at this time. When he got back to England she confronted him with another problem. Milton Greene had been buying antiques in England and shipping them back to America at her expense. Miller advised her to have him fired from the company. As a result she launched legal proceedings against him, accusing him of mismanaging Marilyn Monroe Productions by failing to inform her of secret negotiations he'd entered into with third parties. She replaced him with Miller's brother-in-law George Kupchik.

Greene was shocked to be let go. He claimed he'd devoted over a year of his life to the development of Monroe's career. That meant giving up his own one of photography. Monroe didn't deny this but such "devotion" went too far, she said, citing the fact that he'd made himself executive producer of *The Prince and the Showgirl* as one example of it. He'd been instrumental in giving her autonomy over her career but went too far. It hurt her to lose him and he went quietly from her life. When all the legal wrangles were sorted out he was given $100,000 as a pay-off. It wasn't really apt recompense for all the time he'd put into her. He went back to his photography feeling hard done by.[10]

Nobody knows for sure if he was using the company for his own ends or Monroe's. Neither has it ever been proved if he took money from it on the side. All that's been established for sure is that she got rid of him after Miller expressed his disapproval of him. The same thing had happened with Natasha Lytess. Miller may have been right in both instances or he may not. What's more relevant is the fact that he was taking control of Monroe's life professionally. When the marriage became troubled she felt remorseful about dumping a man who'd been a good friend to her when she was a nobody. She'd lived with both Miller and his wife Amy for some time at their home in Connecticut before her career took off.

The first hint of trouble in the Monroe/Miller marriage occurred when Monroe spotted a note Miller wrote about her one day in London. It suggested he was disappointed in her as a wife.[11] The allegation hurt her deeply. It caused her to have mood swings.

The note also mentioned something about the problems on the film being her fault instead of Olivier. This hurt her almost as much. Up to now she'd always thought he took her side against Olivier.[12]

The notebook may have been left open deliberately. He might have wanted her to try harder at the marriage, to see where she was failing to fulfill him. If so, it backfired. It only incited her aggression against him.

Miller was also said to have written in the note that he could never love Monroe as much as he did the daughter he had by Slattery. According to one of Monroe's biographers he called her a "bitch" in it, or at least suggested she was capable of being one.[13]

Monroe's problems with Olivier weren't helped by the fact that Miller got on with him. At times she felt they were ganging up on her. Olivier was having problems in his own marriage at this time and they weren't unlike Miller's with Monroe. Leigh had become mentally unstable and her mood swings paralleled Monroe's. If Leigh and Monroe could have formed an alliance against the two men it would have leveled the playing field but this was never going to happen. There was too much sexual rivalry between them.

Monroe outshone Olivier in the film. It didn't matter if he enunciated his syllables more eloquently than she did. It wasn't meant to be *Hamlet*. His gifts as a comedian were limited. When she appeared on the screen, all eyes were on her rather than Sir Larry.

# From Story to Film

When Miller and Monroe got back to the U.S. they moved into Miller's country house in Roxbury, Connecticut. A colonial residence dating back to the eighteenth century, he hoped its rustic charm would free Monroe from the constricted goldfish bowl of Hollywood which he felt was sapping her energy.

This was the happiest time of their marriage for Monroe. As well as cooking and cleaning for her new husband she wrote poetry, rode her bicycle along the East River and played tennis. She got to know her new secretary May Reis and her therapist Marianne Kris, who'd been recommended to her by Sigmund Freud's daughter Anna. She slotted herself into the role of the country wife, doing things like hanging pasta over the backs of chairs to drying it with a hair drier. She even bought a book entitled *The Joy of Cooking*.[1] Miller owned a basset hound called Hugo to complete the rural idyll.

Monroe wanted the Roxbury house to be extensively refurbished. To bring this about she employed one of the most famous architects in the world, Frank Lloyd Wright. He was in his nineties by now but still active.

Wright was working on the final stages of the Guggenheim Museum at the time. He met Monroe at the Plaza Hotel and she told him of her plans for the house. She wanted a swimming pool installed as well as a projection booth, an auditorium, a children's nursery and a lavish study for Miller. Such plans would have bankrupted them even if they weren't devised by such a renowned man. In the end they shelved them, opting to renovate the existing house instead.

The renovations caused a lot of disruption. To get away from it they took out a lease on an apartment on 57th Street in New York. They divided their time between that and a cottage they rented near the shore at Amagansett, Long Island. Their life was simple there. They went for walks on the beach and lazed around the cottage.

Miller chipped away at "The Misfits" story to keep himself occupied. Now and then he thought it might make a good film project. As yet it had no female character in it but a girl called Roslyn was mentioned in one of the character's back stories.

One day when they were walking along the beach, Monroe became agitated when she saw some dead fish on the strand. For some reason it brought back a memory to her of a traumatic incident in her childhood when her grandfather (who had severe psychological problems) tried to smother her with a pillow. Miller used the incident as the background for his short story, "Please Don't Kill Anything."[2]

When they got back to Roxbury, Monroe became restless. She seemed to become bored suddenly in her role as a "country wife." The luster of domesticity had worn off. There were too many hours in the day and she had no hobbies. Miller was happy with his own company and was self-contained. He was equally content fixing things around the house as he was writing. Monroe demanded constant attention and became frustrated if he was otherwise engaged. He found it difficult to concentrate on his work under her possessive gaze.

She was somewhat more relaxed in the New York apartment. There were more things to do there and more people to meet, but the electric charge she'd experienced in the early heady days with Miller had dissipated. The luster of that was gone too.

Miller usually got up before Monroe. He had his own bathroom and kept his clothes in a separate closet. According to their maid Lena Pepitone he practically lived in his study. He rarely ventured into her bedroom during the day. He often ate lunch alone and then went out walking with Hugo. Pepitone thought he became more animated talking with May Reis about projects for Monroe than he did talking to Monroe herself.[3]

Even when they were eating together, Pepitone recalled, they didn't talk much. She said Monroe was so exasperated by Miller's distance from her, one day she exploded with the words, "I'm in a fucking prison and my jailer is named Arthur Miller."[4] Monroe's emotions were very close to the surface whereas Miller kept a tight rein on his. No longer did she have a romantic concept of living with a writer. He became boring to her in a similar way to how DiMaggio had some years before. DiMaggio was addicted to television, something Monroe had no time for. She never owned one. With Miller it was his writing desk. She phoned friends and drank Bloody Marys as he tried to overcome a bout of writer's block. He hadn't been able to write plays since he got married. Neither was Monroe overly enthused about any film offers that had been made to her. To the outside world The Writer and The Actress seemed to have it all but behind closed doors they ranged between fire and ice. "When you're both famous," Monroe said, "it's a double problem, even when you're famous in different ways."[5]

She fell pregnant in August, 1957. It was an ectopic pregnancy, the baby being born outside the womb. As such it had no chance of survival. The fetus was removed to save her life. It was the closest she ever came to giving birth as the baby was fully formed. She'd had many miscarriages in the past, including some in the marriage to Miller. A series of botched abortions from the forties has sometimes been given as the reason for this. "This was my last chance," she said to Pepitone.[6]

Miller stayed with her in the hospital. One day she was visited by Sam Shaw, a photographer friend of hers. After chatting with him for a while she suggested he go for a walk with Miller. They walked along by the East River talking about Miller's story. Shaw had read and admired it. He said he thought it would make a great film if he managed to flesh out Roslyn's character. The idea set Miller thinking. Both he and Monroe were feeling very low. Maybe something like that could rouse both of their spirits. What if Monroe were to play Roslyn? It could be a role to get her taken seriously as an actress at last. It might also establish Miller as a screenwriter. He hadn't been able to write through most of their marriage. Monroe's fluctuating moods hadn't helped. He feared the miscarriage could tip her over the edge unless she had something else.

Over the next few days he worked non-stop at adapting the story. He'd never written a screenplay before. He read the dialogue out to Monroe and she liked it. She was amused at the way he put on the voices of the characters as he read it. Even so, she had some reservations about it. Miller had created Rosyln as a kind of erotic waif. She wasn't sure if this would be much of an improvement on the "bubblehead" roles she'd been mired in over the years. Roslyn, she said, was too dependent on the male characters' views of her. She became a "clinging vine."[7]

Monroe was very cautious about what she took on. She'd just signed for *Some Like It Hot*. Miller had encouraged her to. It was a film in which she was called on to accept the ridiculous premise that Jack Lemmon and Tony Curtis were women, after the two took on that disguise following their witnessing a recreation of The St. Valentine's Day Massacre, masterminded by none other than George Raft. In *The Misfits* she thought her character was equally bereft of insight. She was the only cast member who didn't know the horses were going to end up as dog food.

Miller didn't see a problem with either film. In *The Misfits*, how could she be expected to know about the dog food unless she was told? *In Some Like It Hot*, the ignorance was a plot device. It couldn't have worked without her character playing into that. *Some Like It Hot* would turn out to be her most famous film. It takes an intelligent woman to play a dumb one credibly just as it takes a

sober one to play a drunk well. This is what acting is all about. In instances like this, Monroe was really blaming Miller for damage that had been done to her image before he met her.

Apart from the "erotic waif" element, Monroe thought the character of Rosyln was too limited. She felt Miller used aspects of her personality that she'd shared with him in private but failed to expand on them. Her naturalness and "creature of the earth" credentials were catered for but not her dark side. Miller had bypassed that.[8]

Rosyln, as one writer pointed out, isn't so much a character as a quality. A former dancer with no husband or home, she's reached a level of vulnerability where "all things carry the intimation of danger."[9] This was so much like Monroe at this time of her life. Miller would only have needed to turn on a tape recorder during their nights together to write her. He didn't need to be the great author he was.

She'd never had anything written directly for her before. Billy Wilder claimed he had her in mind when he was writing *Some Like It Hot* but that wasn't an original script. She didn't know whether to be flattered or insulted.

Miller tried his best to make his screenplay more credible during the early months of 1958 but he couldn't get out of first gear. The atmosphere was tense between himself and Monroe. They had frequent spats, even in front of visitors like the Strasbergs. When they were alone they didn't have much to say to one another so they tried to entertain as much as they could. Monroe felt out of her depth intellectually on these nights. Some of Miller's friends treated her well but others saw her as "a dull little sex object." They spoke to her "like a high school principal with a backward student."[10]

Monroe started to suffer periodic bouts of depression. She overdosed twice in 1958. On both occasions her stomach was pumped. She was also consuming a lot of alcohol. One day she fell down a flight of stairs while she was drinking, cutting her wrist on the glass.[11]

She continued to attend the Actors Studio. The terms "Marilyn Monroe" and "Actors Studio" might have struck some people as antithetical but she was completely committed to its ideals and gave herself over to them totally. She also did fundraisers for Joe Strasberg. Some people thought he was exploiting her.[12]

Strasberg was like Monroe's "umbilical cord" to the Actors Studio.[13] "I had to find the real me," she said, "outside my looks, which people were hung up on." [14] She wanted to play Lady Macbeth opposite Marlon Brando's Macbeth. [15]

Strasberg saw something in her that most other acting coaches missed. "What was going on inside was not what was going on outside," he said. "That always means there may be something there to work with." Of all the stars he worked with, he said, Monroe and Marlon Brando were the two who stood out for him.[16] One of the reasons Strasberg took such an interest in Monroe was to rebuild his reputation.[17] It suffered some damage from Brando's renunciation of him in favor of Stella Adler.

Under Strasberg, Monroe embraced the Stanislavsky concept of improvisation as the best way of getting inside a character's skin. She tapped into her "sense memory" to inflate scripts.

Joan Crawford was the most vociferous critic of such lofty ambitions. "I have just come from the Actors Studio," she said one day, "where I saw Marilyn Monroe. She had no girdle on. Her ass was hanging out. She is a disgrace to the industry."[18]

Billy Wilder was equally dismissive of this aspect of her. The best school she could go to, he advised, was one that taught her how to show up in places on time.[19] He said this as a result of the frustration he endured with her on *Some Like It Hot*, her next film after *The Prince and the Showgirl*. Monroe was exceptionally difficult on the set of this film, causing immense frustration to her costars Jack Lemmon and Tony Curtis and also to Wilder. Paula Strasberg almost doubled as a second director for her. She used to try and get into the moods for scenes. She found it difficult to remember lines because she was trying to filter them through the Stanislavsky template of linking them in with her emotional state.

Miller thought interfering with scripts was a dangerous road for her to go down. Words, he argued, had been important in her most successful films, films like *Some Like It Hot*. Improvising wasn't fair on the other actors either. It meant she would be throwing them different cues.

Monroe didn't listen when he talked to her like that. She decided she wasn't going to be a bimbo anymore. She wouldn't be someone who got to the top because her dresses didn't. She wanted to play Grushenka in *The Brothers Karamazov*.

Miller wasn't the only one who thought she was playing with fire by discovering all the qualities that had got her to where she

was. Clifford Odets was also aware of the danger the Actors Studio posed for her. "I hope my old Group Theater buddies don't make her too self-conscious," he said.[20]

She thought she was under-used by Hollywood. "If I were a car," she said to Strasberg, "they'd be driving me in low gear. That's bad for the engine and depressing for the car.[21]

Her presence at the Actors Studio generated a lot of interest. Everyone wanted to know what the studio had that interested the "phosphorescent" Marilyn. [22] She never became an official mem-

*Both Monroe and Miller, seen here with John Huston, had great respect for the veteran director.*

ber.[23] Even so, she performed many interesting pieces there, from *Golden Boy* to *A Streetcar Named Desire* to Molly Bloom's soliloquy from James Joyce's *Ulysses*. No doubt this was the biggest stretch for her.

Susan Strasberg witnessed it. She said she did it in a black velvet dress that captured Bloom's "real sexuality." She'd dispensed with "the whispery Hollywood mask" for "an earthy, longing, resilient woman."[24]

Was she ready to play Roslyn in *The Misfits*? She thought so – at least if Miller could resist the temptation to write her as herself.

If it became a film, she wanted John Huston to direct it. He'd been kind to Monroe during the shooting of her 1950 feature, *The Asphalt Jungle*. He saw something in her that other directors hadn't. The film put her on the road to movie success and maybe even saved her from a life of couch casting. She'd been dropped from Fox at the time.[25] Huston saw her potential and gave her a screen test. Everything followed after that. Monroe always regarded it as one of her best performances.[26] She also thought it was Huston's best film.[27]

Monroe had been nervous on *The Asphalt Jungle* but Huston relaxed her. He told her to look at Louis Calhern, another actor in the film who was more established than she was. "See how he's shaking," he said, "If you're not nervous you might as well give up."[28]

Huston's style of direction was muted. "I tell an actor as little as possible," he said. "When I have to step in I feel defeated."[29] Monroe admired this in him. He wasn't just a director. He was an actor and a writer as well. And he painted. In many ways he saw his films as paintings. His style of direction was courteous but distant. He believed actors shouldn't be told how to act. They should "pull it out of themselves."[30] She knew he wouldn't make *The Misfits* kitsch or "pleasant."[31] He'd go for the inner truth.

Miller worked on the screenplay now with a renewed sense of zeal. The first concrete thing he needed to do was find a producer. He invited Frank Taylor to his house in Roxbury. Taylor wasn't a producer but Miller felt he could become one if the film materialized. They were friends from publishing. Taylor had edited Miller's only novel, *Focus*, when he worked for the publishers Reynal & Hitchcock. In 1948 he'd become a Hollywood producer. He was blacklisted during the McCarthy era. That necessitated his return to publishing. Now Miller wanted him to merge the two worlds. They decided to do a reading of the screenplay in Miller's house.

Taylor brought his wife and three sons with him. Monroe was nervous when they arrived. She stayed upstairs vacuuming the carpet. When she finally came down she focused most of her attention on Taylor's sons, especially the most quiet one, Mark. Taylor's wife helped her make lunch but the reading went on so long it ended up getting burned.

Taylor liked the screenplay. He told Miller to send it to Huston. He gave him his address in Ireland. Huston had a baronial mansion there. It was where he retired to in order to escape the rigors of film making, one of his many international bolt holes. He hadn't made a film in Hollywood for eight years.

In a letter he attached to the script, Miller mentioned that Monroe would be available to play the part of Roslyn. She'd also been

*Roslyn shows the menfolk of Reno how to really shake that bat.*

considering the role of Holly Golightly in *Breakfast at Tiffany's* at this point. Truman Capote, who wrote it, thought she'd be more suitable for it than Audrey Hepburn. Hepburn was in the running for the part. Truman had written Holly as a lady of the night. Hepburn would go on to play the role and sanitize it. Monroe was also tinkering with the idea of appearing in *Paris Blues* with Marlon Brando. (Neither of them appeared in that film.)

After writing to Huston, Miller sent a copy of the script to Elia Kazan. He'd had a fractious relationship with Kazan over the years, not only because he'd impregnated Monroe when Miller was dating her – the baby was aborted – but, more significantly, because Kazan had "named names" to HUAC during the communist witch hunt.

Huston wrote back to Miller in a letter that was short and to the point: "Dear Arthur, Script magnificent, Regards, John."[32] So it was going to be a film. Miller was over the moon. At this time Huston was also working on a script written by Jean-Paul Sartre about Sigmund Freud. This was several hundred pages long and in much need of pruning. Huston was glad to be able to put it aside to concentrate on Miller's infinitely more economical work. In October, Miller wrote to Huston again to tell him he was excited to be approaching the "big day" when filming would start.[33]

Huston was interested in Robert Mitchum taking the lead role in the film. He sent him the screenplay but Mitchum didn't like it. He told his agent, "If John Huston calls, tell him I died."[34] Huston met Mitchum in London shortly afterwards. He said he was disappointed Mitchum hadn't got back to him about the screenplay. Mitchum said it made no sense to him. Huston said he could have it changed if Mitchum wished. Mitchum then said he heard Huston thought it was magnificent. Huston was caught out. He told him he was thinking of Clark Gable for it. Mitchum said he heard Gable was on two quarts of whisky a day, that the action scenes would kill him.[35] How prescient that was.

Miller now tried to get Gable on board. Gable read his script but, like Mitchum, he didn't really understand the point of it. He was told it was going to be a western but it didn't sound like one. Miller said, "It's an eastern western." Gable's interest was aroused at this. Miller said traditional westerns were too cut and dried for him, that this was a different type of one. There were no cliched heroes or villains. In *The Misfits*, he said the good guy was even part of the problem. Gable said he'd consider it. At 59, he was ready for a challenge.[36]

Montgomery Clift was now thought of for the second male lead. He was a good friend of Monroe's. He'd been offered a part in one of Monroe's recent films, *Bus Stop*, but he turned it down. It went to Don Murray instead. Clift admired Monroe's performance. He got to know her better when she was making *Some Like It Hot*.

She was in denial about his homosexuality. The idea of him sleeping with another man struck her as weird: "Why would he do that? He could have any girl in the world." He was also good friends with Elizabeth Taylor. Monroe presumed he'd slept with her. She always regarded Taylor as a rival for his affections.[37]

Clift was a fan of Miller's work. He'd been to see *Death of a Salesman* and was excited by it. After he came out of the theatre he gushed, "It was fantastic! He's saying the American Dream is full of shit!"[38] He loved *The Misfits* script when he read it. "It's a

Gable Monroe Clift in The John Huston Production the Misfits Thelma Ritter Eli Wallach Arthur Miller Frank E. Taylor John Huston

wonderful part," he said of the character he would be playing. "If I don't do it justice I'll shoot myself." [39]

There were insurance problems for both Clift and Gable. Both of them failed their physical exams. Gable was told to give up smoking and to reduce his weight to 195 pounds. At this time he weighed 230 pounds. He'd just come back from Italy where he'd made *It Started in Naples* with Sophia Loren. He blamed his weight on all the pasta she'd cooked for him.

Clift was drinking heavily when he signed for the film. He often engaged in self-destructive behavior when he was drinking. This was intensified after a car crash nearly killed him in 1956. He had plastic surgery on his face and he was paralyzed down one side. He nearly choked to death in the crash. Two teeth lay lodged in his throat before Elizabeth Taylor pulled them out. They were in the middle of making *Raintree County* at the time.

Clift's friend Kevin McCarthy had been in the car ahead of him on the night of the accident. They were leaving a party thrown by Taylor. He visited Clift the next night in hospital. "He looked like a David Levine cartoon," he said. "His face ballooned up to six times its normal size. He was propped up in bed unable to speak because his jaw was wired. His eyes glared out at me helplessly."[40]

The accident traumatized Clift in a way he could never admit to anyone. His once perfect nose and mouth were off-kilter, his upper lip jutting over his lower one. Every so often, according to one of his biographers, he covered his face with his hands "like someone who'd been terrified by a flesh-crawling horror movie."[41]

When *Raintree County* came out he hated it. Much of his disdain related to his appearance. He thought audiences would look at him and wonder which scenes were shot before the accident and which ones after it. "In my beard," he said, "I look like Jesus Christ in a union cap."[42]

The accident would have been traumatic for anyone but for someone as vulnerable as Clift it was life-changing. Edward Dmytryk, the director of *Raintree County*, said of him, "Monty was the most sensitive man I've ever known. If somebody kicked a dog a mile away he'd feel it."[43] He often played down his good looks, thinking of them as secondary to his talent – and sometimes getting in the way of it – but he also knew they were any actor's meal ticket. Without them he feared his career would suffer greatly.

One of the reasons he accepted the film was because of the shortness of his part. Like Monroe he always had difficulty learning dialogue and keeping his concentration going for long stretches on the set. He told Henderson Cleaves of the World-Telegram & Sun: "I decided to do *The Misfits* because I don't appear on the screen until page 57."[44]

The cast was rounded off with Eli Wallach, Thelma Ritter and Kevin McCarthy. They were all Actors Studio members. Wallach and Ritter needed no introduction. They may not have always been lead performers but everyone knew their pedigree. McCarthy had starred with Clift in a stage version of *The Seagull*.

Taylor was delighted to have assembled such star performers. He contacted Lew Wasserman, the head of MCA, and he proved equally enthusiastic. Wasserman secured financing from United Artists. Taylor knew this studio was ideal for the film. It was based in Greenwich Village and put aesthetic concerns before commercial ones.[45]

*Clark Gable was initially reluctant to appear in the film when Huston first approached him with the project but once he committed to it he gave it everything.*

Taylor demanded autonomy in his new role. He asked to be paid by United Artists rather than by Miller and Monroe. "I'm not going to be captive to you," he told them. "Either I'm paid by UA or not at all. I have to be free to state my opinion."[46] As an employee of Marilyn Monroe Productions he didn't think he'd be able to do that. Huston wanted to shoot the film in Mexico for tax reasons but

Miller told him that would destroy its mood. It had to be Reno, he insisted. Taylor agreed and Huston was finally won round.[47]

Miller and Taylor scouted locations for the film in December, 1959. They re-visited the Stix house in Reno where Miller met the three Mustangers. Dayton, a ghost town south of Virginia City, was selected as the location for a rodeo scene in the film. The climax was going to be shot at Pyramid Lake, a fifteen mile stretch of dry lake where the wild horses were going to be drawn away from the mountains and trapped.

Despite his age and physical condition, Gable demanded a salary of $750,000 and ten per cent of the gross. He also asked for $48,000 a week overtime. This would prove especially lucrative to him because of all the delays that occurred on the film, most of them due to Monroe. She was delighted he was going to be in it. She'd only met him once. It was at a party in the fifties. She danced with him, entranced to be in the arms of a man she'd idolized all her life. The Love God of yesteryear and the Love Goddess of the present were about to star together for the first time.

Monroe regarded Gable as a father figure to her. When she was a child, her mother gave her a picture of him to pass off as her missing father.[48] She was placed in an orphanage after her mother developed psychological problems. The idea of Gable being her father seemed even more important then. "I became very close to that face," she said. "He became my fantasy. I dreamed of seeing him on the street." Now he was even closer than that. She was making a film with him: "I'll have him all to myself."[49]

Well, not exactly. He was deeply in love with his third wife, Kay. They were expecting their first child together. But Monroe was always good at fantasizing. She could pretend her screen lover was her real life one with some Method projection.

# L.A. Interlude

Before Monroe could begin *The Misfits* she had to fulfill a commitment to Twentieth Century-Fox with the George Cukor musical comedy *Let's Make Love*. Her co-star was the French actor Yves Montand. Montand was anxious to spread his wings outside his native country. He was married to Simone Signoret. Both of them had appeared in Miller's play *The Crucible* in Paris in 1953. The Salem witch hunts in the play became a metaphor for the red-baiting of Senator Joseph McCarthy during the HUAC investigations. Both Montand and Signoret had, like Miller, leftwing orientations. Montand's father had been an activist against Mussolini during World War II.

Various stars were considered for the lead before Montand. Cary Grant wasn't interested. Rock Hudson was unavailable. The money wasn't enough for Charlton Heston. Gregory Peck spent a few days on the set but then departed. Already he saw Monroe was too much of a diva for him to be able to breathe.[1] He hadn't liked the film either, finding it "about as funny as pushing Grandma down the stairs."[2]

Miller first met Montand in Paris in 1956 when he was having problems with HUAC. In three short years he'd gone from being seen as a possible political subversive to a darling of the left. His problems with getting a visa to leave the U.S. were long over. Now Montand was trying to get one to stay there. Getting a foothold in Hollywood was important to expedite this.

Miller and Monroe went to live in Los Angeles at the beginning of 1960. They were assigned a bungalow adjacent to the one occupied by Montand and Signoret at the Beverly Hills Hotel. There was a lot of traffic between bungalows 20 and 21 at this time. The couples had become friendly during the staging of *The Crucible*. In fact it was largely due to Monroe's influence that Montand landed the role in the film. She strengthened her friendship with him on

the set and with Signoret off it. She made pasta with Signoret in the evenings and went shopping with her on the weekends. They had their hair bleached together as Miller continued to beaver away at *The Misfits* screenplay.

Montand was more friendly with Miller than Monroe at this point. He was aware of her reputation as a sexbomb. He was attracted to her, but even though cracks were beginning to show in her marriage to Miller he deemed her off-limits. His marriage to Signoret wasn't lily white but neither Miller nor Signoret saw Monroe as a threat. This despite that fact that she told a journalist before the cameras rolled for *Let's Make Love* that she regarded Montand as the most attractive man she'd ever met next to Miller and Marlon Brando.[3] He was the kind of man she was attracted to – older and in some ways slightly craggy.

Alex Finlayson wrote a "filmic drama" called *The Misfits*. In one of the scenes, a character says of Monroe, "She fell for Montand because he resembled Joe DiMaggio. If you put Montand, DiMaggio and Miller in baseball suits and sent them out to left field, you wouldn't be able to tell them apart."[4]

Miller and Montand became good friends. They went out walking many evenings as their wives bonded. Walking wasn't something people did in the "all vehicle" culture of Beverly Hills. Once or twice they were even stopped by policemen inquiring as to what they were doing.

Monroe found *Let's Make Love* beneath her. Fired up with Method aspirations from her sojourns at the Actors Studio, she asked Miller if he could inject some substance into it. He was happy to comply after its producer Spyros Skouras made it worth his while financially with a $25,000 check. Having said that, he didn't enjoy the task. How could he make something out of a script that was in essence banal? He would have had to throw it out altogether and start from nothing. Obviously that wasn't feasible. He did his best to doctor it to address his wife's concerns.

Shooting of the film was interrupted by an actors' strike. They were protesting against not having been paid residuals from television broadcasts of their films. It was amazing that Miller disrespected their grievance to the extent he did by working through the strike and thus undermining its legitimacy. Where was his left wing conscience now?

Miller didn't mention in his autobiography that he was paid so handsomely for *Let's Make Love* or that he breached the strike to do it. All he said was that he was taking on the re-write to save Monroe "from a complete catastrophe."[5] Montand saw a contradiction in the fact that Miller complained about prostituting his art while pocketing the hefty check.[6]

Producer Robert Whitehead once said of Miller, "He liked money more than a good left-winger was supposed to."[7]. It was a charge Monroe also leveled at him when things started to go wrong between them.

He didn't ask for a credit for his work. One reason was because he didn't think much of it. Another was the fact that he wanted *The Misfits* to be listed as his screenwriting debut.[8]

Miller's re-writes didn't do much to improve the script. Comedy was never his forte and that was what was called for in this instance. Monroe wasn't happy with what he did. She took her dissatisfaction out on both Miller and Cukor.

Miller tried to downplay the fluctuations in her moods during *Let's Make Love* just as he had during *The Prince and the Showgirl* and *Some Like It Hot*. He asked the respective directors to make allowances for her. This proved easier with Cukor ("the women's director") and Laurence Olivier (who was a friend of his) than it had been with Wilder. At times he felt more like Monroe's agent than her husband. There were that many interventions on her behalf during the shoot.

Nominations for the Oscars were announced at the end of March. Signoret received one for playing Laurence Harvey's tragic mistress in Jack Clayton's powerful adaptation of John Braine's novel *Room at the Top*. It was regarded as unusual for a French actress to be honored at the Oscars, especially in a low-budget British feature. Her left wing political stance was also expected to come against her. But she won. Monroe always predicted she would. Monroe herself hadn't been nominated despite getting some of the best notices of her career for *Some Like It Hot*.

She deserved at least a nomination for the film. Why did she not receive one? There were various theories, one of which was that she'd made too many enemies in the Academy over the years due to her persistent demands and unpredictable behavior. This came against her even more than Signoret's liberalism.

Miller now went to Ireland to work on *The Misfits* screenplay with Huston. Montand and Monroe both felt artistically challenged by their spouses. Would they now embark on the relationship that had been subtly threatened from Day One of their meeting? Miller didn't seem to care if they did. His parting words to Montand were, "What will happen will happen." It was almost as if he was donating his wife to him. Montand was shocked. Doris Vidor, the widow of the director Charles Vidor and a friend to both of them, thought Miller went to Ireland deliberately to throw the pair together.[9]

Huston met Miller in Ireland. They liked one another from the start. Huston was limping at the time. He'd broken his leg after having tried to scale a five foot wall.

Miller was impressed by the elegance of his home. It was located in Craughwell, Galway. He called it St. Clarens. "Ireland is the reverse of every country in the world," Huston told Miller. "That's why I live here." The talk turned to Miller's screenplay. Huston understood it right off. He told Miller he thought it was about people who sold their work but refused to sell their lives: "That's why they're misfits." Miller said, "Now I know what it's about!" They discussed the script before a roaring fire over several bottles of Irish whisky. Miller felt he was working with another writer rather than a director.[10]

Before he left L.A. he'd asked Montand and Signoret to look after Monroe. Signoret perhaps overdid this. She spent the following night telling her stories. Monroe was intrigued by them. It was after midnight before they went to bed. Montand had been studying his lines and retired early. Monroe had a 5 a.m. start the next day. She stayed up despite Signoret urging her to go back to her apartment.

She slept it out the following morning. Montand became frustrated waiting for her at the studio. He rang Signoret to ask her if she knew why Monroe hadn't turned up. Signoret went to Monroe's apartment to try and find out. She knocked but there was no answer.

Montand left the set. He went to her apartment but he received no answer either. He wrote a note to her and slipped it under the door. It said, "You can do what you like to Spyros Skouras and the Fox Studio and all the producers in town if that's what you want. But the next time you decide to hang around listening to my wife telling you stories instead of going to bed because you've already

decided not to get up the next morning and go to the studio, please tell me. Don't leave me to work for hours on end on a scene you've already decided not to do the next day. I'm not the enemy. I'm your pal. Capricious little girls have never amused me."[11]

Monroe was devastated when she read the note. She rang Miller and asked him to intervene. He rang the Montands. "Be gentle with her," he implored. They went around to her apartment again. This time she was in tears. "I'm bad," she said, "I won't do it again." She was like a child who'd misbehaved and was now throwing herself on her parents' mercy. Signoret was highly amused by the whole incident. "She phoned Dublin," she said, "so Dublin would phone her next-door neighbors."[12] It was classic Monroe.

Worse was to come. One night when Monroe lay in bed suffering from one of her familiar bouts of exhaustion, Montand called to try and prop up her spirits. They exchanged pleasantries for a few minutes. Afterwards he bent down to kiss her goodnight. She turned her head and made the kiss into something much more passionate. A fire was lit for both of them. The inevitable affair had begun.

Montand was like her consolation prize for not being nominated for *Some Like It Hot.* As she said once, "A career is a wonderful thing but you can't snuggle up to it on a cold night."[13] Signoret may have had the Oscar but Monroe had Montand.

On set they were professional and discreet. In the evenings it was easy to slip from Bungalow 20 to 21 and go where their sexual appetites led them. It was Montand's first time cheating on his wife. He tried to rationalize it by saying things about Monroe like, "She had a kind of innocence. The less she tried, the more attractive it was."[14] More frankly he confessed, "I was alone in Hollywood for five months and I'm no saint. Who could resist Marilyn Monroe?"[15]

Monroe took it all much more seriously than he did as the film rumbled to a close. Then the press got hold of it. Would it end the Monroe/Miller marriage? Would it end the Montand/Signoret one? All sorts of stories started to appear.

Miller didn't seem to care one way or the other. His focus was more on *The Misfits* now than his marriage. Montand had similar priorities. He embarked on the romance, he said, to help him with his part.[16]

Both Miller and Signoret seemed to give Montand a carte blanche to have an affair with Monroe because she was, as Montand said, irresistible. Neither of them thought he'd stay with her. That was their main worry.

Monroe was beautiful, Montand told *Ici-Paris*, but it was Signoret that he loved.[17] Monroe was dismissed as a homewrecker by the French press while Miller observed a heroic silence. *Paris-Match* wrote, "The Montands have survived Hurricane Marilyn."[18]

Stories about the affair sold newspapers so journalists continued to ratchet up the drama with sensational lies. Montand and Signoret were rumored to be fighting, to be boarding planes for different countries. Miller, meanwhile, slept with his typewriter rather than Monroe.

Some writers speculated that she started the affair to see if he would be bothered by it. The fact that he didn't bridle against it suggested he'd already given up on their long-term prospects.[19]

Montand never gave Monroe cause to think he'd leave Signoret for her. He'd had strings of lovers in the past but always went home to his wife. It was like an open marriage, at least on his part.[20]

Signoret was more fatalistic. If Monroe liked her husband, she said, it showed what good taste he had.[21] She didn't speak much about the affair, observing a dignified silence like Miller, but maybe her silence spoke louder than words. Her friend Catherine Deneuve

said she had Monroe etched on her face "like a permanent scar."[22] What bothered her most wasn't the moral violation as much as the humiliation.[23] And of course the fear of losing Montand forever.

"Not for a moment did I think of breaking with my wife," Montand declared, "but if she had slammed the door on me, I would probably have made my life with Marilyn. Or tried to. That was the direction we were moving in. Maybe it would only have lasted two or three years. I didn't have too many illusions. Still, what years they would have been!"[24] His comments betray the fact that he was content to let Signoret go without a fight if she threw him out. And, more alarmingly, that Monroe was little more than a plaything to him to be used and abused as he saw fit.

Montand stayed in Hollywood after *Let's Make Love* wrapped. Monroe went to New York and tried to keep away from the media storm.

The American press got going on Monroe/Montand gossip. Twentieth Century-Fox was delighted. Now maybe they'd be able to sell their silly little film after all. There were stories in the tabloids that Monroe had turned up at Montand's bungalow dressed in nothing but a fur coat, that Miller had found them in bed together after he returned unexpectedly to the building to get his pipe.[25] The stories had all the ingredients of an airport novel. *Let's Make Love* indeed.

On June 30, Montand had to stop in New York for a plane change on his way back to Paris. Monroe met him at the airport to try and continue their relationship. She even booked a room for the pair of them in a nearby hotel. Her behavior was presumptuous. He refused to go to the hotel room with her. Instead they sat in the back of a limousine drinking champagne. He told her in no uncertain terms that their relationship was finished, that he was going back to Signoret. He was about to make a film called *Sanctuary*. Monroe was getting ready for *The Misfits*. It was back to business for both of them.

Monroe accepted what she couldn't change. She acted as if everything was normal, even finding time to congratulate Signoret on her Oscar.

She didn't see a disjunction in being friends with Signoret after bedding her husband any more than she saw a disjunction between living with Miller in a relationship that was rocky as they embarked on a film together. Fred Guiles saw this not as duplicity but "a neat splitting of self." [26]

Everything seemed upside down. The sex symbol fell in love with a man who used her for her body but permanence was more important to her than to him.

She was accustomed to getting her way in relationships, accustomed to drawing men away from their wives. Now she had to learn to take defeat. There was a film to be made – with a man she didn't love anymore. Montand, meanwhile, went back to his old life. His enemies saw him as someone who seduced Monroe and then abandoned her to barbiturates and the Nevada desert. [27]

# Arrival in Reno

Monroe left New York on July 17 to fly to Nevada. Her friend James Haspiel saw her off at the airport. He was shocked by her "ravaged" face, so much so that he had to turn away from her. There were menstrual stains on her skirt. He took them to be caused by one of the painful periods he knew her to suffer from. She had bags under her eyes as well.[1]

She arrived in Reno three days later. Miller met her. She looked bloated and tired. There were twenty people at the airport. She kept them waiting a half hour as she changed her clothes in the plane lavatory. It was the sign of things to come.

Several local VIPs were there to greet her. Councilman Charles Cowen gave her the keys to the city as a gesture of goodwill. She did her best to put on a happy face but the body language between herself and Miller was bad. They left the airport in separate cars. When Miller arrived at the Mapes Hotel, which was where they were going to be staying for the duration of the shoot, he was asked for an autograph as "Marilyn Monroe's husband" rather than as himself.[2]

Monroe was agitated when she reached the Mapes. She usually had time to recharge her batteries between films but in this case, because of the strike delaying the finish date of *Let's Make Love*, there was no chance of that. *The Misfits* was originally supposed to start shooting in May. That would have been more to everyone's taste. They were now in the height of the summer. Temperatures had reached 130 degrees. That would have been bad enough anywhere else but in Nevada, where it was often difficult to catch one's breath at the best of times, it was exponentially worse. Huston suffered more than anyone as he was a heavy smoker and he had emphysema. The desert was the last place he should have been with his hacking cough.

Monroe asked him if he could delay starting the film. "Please," she said to him, "I'm exhausted. I'm 34 years old and I've been singing and dancing for five months on that lousy picture. I need time to get my spirits up."[3] Huston couldn't agree to that. He'd lost too much time already. The cameras had to roll immediately.

The other cast members apart from Monroe, Gable, Clift, Wallach and Ritter were James Barton, Estelle Winwood and Kevin McCarthy. McCarthy is the man Monroe is divorcing at the beginning of the film. She knew most of these people from The Actors Studio. Clift and McCarthy had been special friends there before Clift's car crash. They'd even gone to Europe on holiday together in 1951. They shared an apartment while they were there, leading to rumors that they'd had a gay relationship. These were false. McCarthy didn't even know Clift was gay at the time.

Their relationship cooled as Clift's drinking problem increased. By the time of *The Misfits* it had almost totally petered out. In fact Clift had now come to believe McCarthy used him to get ahead in his career.[4] McCarthy had only 27 words in the script. His agent was against him doing it until he was guaranteed a special mention in the credits.

McCarthy also knew Monroe from the Actors Studio. He remembered her doing a scene from Chekhov's *Three Sisters* once. She looked tousled and ordinary before she went onto the stage but then metamorphosed into something transcendent.[5]

Most of the cast were more upbeat than Monroe. Gable had gone on a crash diet to satisfy his insurers and lost 35 pounds. He was on the set with his third wife, Kay Williams. She was significantly younger than him and very outdoorsy. They played golf together and fished and shot. He'd just bought a new Mercedes at her urging. He showed it off to the other cast members with the enthusiasm of an adolescent. He said he was determined to break speed records every day on his way to work. In the evenings he swam in the pool of the house they were renting. The golf course was beside it. He'd cut down on his drinking. Life was good as he approached his fifth wedding anniversary with Kay. She had children from previous marriages and was now pregnant with his first one.

Gable didn't try and pretend the role was any kind of romantic lead. "My days of playing the dashing young lover are over," he declared. "I'm no longer believable in those parts. There has been considerable talk about older guys wooing and winning leading ladies half their age. I don't think the public likes it and I don't care for it myself. It's not realistic. The actresses I started going out with have long since quit playing glamour girls and sweet young things. Now it's time I acted my age."[6]

In fact he always did. Despite his credentials as "The King of Hollywood", he liked to demythologize himself. He once fended off a woman who made advances on him by taking out his false teeth and flashing them in front of her. It cooled her ardor.[7]

Even though some of the material was solemn, he approached it lightly: "The public come to the movies to see Gable as Gable. They don't want to see me pulling any tricks and getting serious on 'em."[8] Miller hadn't written the part specifically for him but after meeting him he knew he was ideal for it.[9] The fact that Monroe liked him so much also helped.

Her fondness for him wasn't surprising. Apart from the fact of thinking he was her actual father when she was young, her attraction to older men fed into their screen chemistry. There was a cragginess about him, the look of a man who'd lived.

She'd only met him once before. It was at a party at Romanoff's to celebrate the completion of *The Seven Year Itch*. She danced with him and told him she'd always wanted to be in a film with him.[10] Now she was.

Monroe was delighted to see Clift too. They'd got drunk together one night in New York the previous year. He was filming *Lonely Hearts* and she *Some Like It Hot*. Both of them were frustrated with their performances. They were always able to unload their problems on one another, to see in each other a mirror image of each other.

Clift hadn't had a successful film for some time. People were saying his career was over now that his looks were gone. He also had problems with his eyes. He had cataracts and was worried about going blind.

*Miller was rarely seen without his pipe on the set. Gable was on a health kick on doctor's orders after a lifetime of smoking.*

Wallach was nervous seeing him. The last time they'd met was at a party in New York. Clift had just had his plastic surgery following the car accident. He thought Wallach was avoiding him for that reason. Wallach was wearing a Burberry trench coat with military epaulets. Clift walked over to him and tore off one of them. "That's for failing to recognize a fellow actor," he said. Wallach was astonished. He felt like punching him. The reason he didn't was because he felt sorry for him. Clift cooled down. He told him to have his tailor sew the epaulet back on, that he'd pay for it.[11]

Wallach was a long time friend of Monroe. He first met her when he was appearing on stage in *The Teahouse of August Moon* on Broadway. She was interested in him teaching her about stagecraft. He later introduced her to James Joyce's *Ulysses.* This intrigued her. As far as the press was concerned, Wallach was little more than a "beard" who went around with her to deflect press attention from Miller, whom she'd then just started dating. The reality was that they were close friends. He more than anyone else was instrumental in Monroe attending the Actors Studio.[12]

He also knew the other side of her, the one that was a million miles away from serious acting. He was with her on the night in the summer of 1955 when the 40-foot high poster of her posing above a ventilator was unveiled prior to the opening of *The Seven Year Itch*. "That's the way they think of me," she complained to him, "with my skirt over my head." "She didn't seem to mind," Wallach said. "She accepted it."[13]

Since then he'd heard rumors that she's become troubled, that her marriage was on the rocks because of her relationship with Montand. He was apprehensive about running into her again.[14]

He needn't have worried. At a pre-shoot party thrown by Taylor she was friendly with him. "Arthur has written a wonderful scene for us," she said to him, "and we dance too. I'm so happy we'll be working together."[15]

Gable hadn't wanted to go to the party. He knew Clift and Wallach were Method actors and that bothered him. He had no time for the Method. All he had to do was look in a mirror and he became the character he was playing.[16] He drew on his memories for his performances: "I gather up everything I was, everything I am and everything I hope to be. That's about it."[17] Clift thought he lacked range for that reason.[18] At the party, however, they all got along fine. Kay had encouraged Gable to go to it and he was glad he did. It broke the ice between all of them.

Even though the Monroe/Miller marriage was in crisis, Miller felt confident the two of them could last through the months of filming because of the happy atmosphere between the cast and crew. Monroe was surrounded by people she liked and got on with – Gable, Clift, Wallach and Ritter, a special friend of hers from the Actors Studio. She also had her masseur Ralph Roberts, her press secretary May Reis, her makeup man Allan "Whitey" Snyder, her stand-in Evelyn Moriarty, her limo driver Rudy Kausky, her publicist Rupert Allan and the two people who did her hair, Sidney Guilaroff and Agnes Flanagan. Reis had worked for Miller in the past. Huston gave Roberts a small part as an ambulance driver in the film.

The only person Huston was concerned about was Paula Strasberg, who replaced Natasha Lytess as Monroe's acting coach and who threatened to derail any production with her imperiousness. For

*Monroe always had great affection for children, which made it all the more tragic that she could never have any of her own. Here she's horsing around with a lad who appeared on the set as her acting coach Paula Strasberg – Black Bart – ruminates in the background.*

years directors had to put with Lytess undercutting their authority. They greeted her departure with glee. Little did they anticipate the fact that her replacement would exercise an even more substantial influence on Monroe.

Strasberg was a failed actress. She'd once been tested for a role but Joan Blondell got it instead. In Monroe she tried to recapture her own career vicariously.[19] In time she became like her shadow. People joked that they almost went to the bathroom together. She discussed everything with her: how she should walk, how she should speak, what might inspire her to play a scene better. It was disconcerting for directors to have to deal with this. Strasberg became like a surrogate director to her. As such, she often second-guessed what the actual director did. On the set of *Some Like It Hot*, Billy Wilder used to say to her, "How was that for you, Paula?" after takes.

Strasberg always dressed in black – black dress, black jacket, black stockings, black shoes, black hat and black veil. She said she did so to be inconspicuous. It had the opposite effect. It must have been severely uncomfortable in the 130 degree heat. The crew called her "Black Bart" because of her apparel. None of them knew she was in the early stages of bone cancer. All they knew was that she was eccentric. She wore multiple watches so she could tell what all the actors she was mentoring might be doing in various corners of the globe.[20] Coincidentally, her maiden name was Miller.

# Shooting Begins

The production finally got under way. It was exactly two years since Frank Taylor had visited Miller and listened to him imitating the voices of the cowboys as Monroe vacuumed the upstairs room of their house.

The Nevada setting of the film was suitable for its theme of weather-beaten souls trying to find their anchors in an uncertain universe. Miller once said that in this state you could spend a whole day without seeing anyone. It was a land from which all grace seemed to have been withdrawn "except for a certain beauty menaced by modernity."[1] His story was about powerlessness, he said, and Nevada was "the center of common loss."[2] As Fred Guiles put it, "It was a graveyard of abandoned mines and silver boom towns that had died; a place of nature's fossils as well."[3]

Miller tried to capture its essence in his screenplay rather than the bland locale it had become in many people's eyes, a place where there were even slot machines in supermarkets. People dropped coins in them, he said, in the same way they might discard a Kleenex.[4]

It was "a land of shadows," Fred Guiles wrote, "a graveyard for prehistoric mammoths, a dead place for played-out mines."[5] What better location, then, for a tale of four wasted souls trying to grab a foothold on what might loosely be termed Normal Life?

The Reno atmosphere hardly conduced to marital bliss. Nearly 5000 divorces had been granted there the previous year. Both Miller and Monroe knew how the game worked. The film was like a dress rehearsal for it, a semi-fictional gambit that spilled over into their lives. W.J. Weatherby wrote: "You could see the ex-wives emerge from the legal offices and courtrooms tossing their wedding rings into the Truckee River like prisoners losing their chains. Adultery, cruelty, desertion, alcoholism, non-support; the reasons for ending the marriages were ticked off as unemotionally as the Dow-Jones

average. If the gamblers in the casinos seemed to work by automation, so did the divorcing couples. You could see them at all hours of the day or night, whiling away the six weeks they had to be there to qualify for their divorce – perched over cards, spinning wheels or working the one-armed bandits."[6]

Reno is where everything ends. Marriages are dissolved in the courts and fortunes lost in the casinos. Horses lose their lives in mustanging. All that's left is for their capturers to lose their souls. Unless someone like Rosyln, a tainted saint, can redeem them.

In the desert outside Reno, Miller wrote, "Night begins a few inches off the ground. In a sterile white alkali waste the desolation is almost supernatural. There is no tree, no bush, no pool of water. To right and left the blank white flatland stretches away, dampened here and there by acrid stains of moisture left from spring rains. Gradually a perverse beauty grows out of the place. Its ugliness is so direct and blatant as to take on the honesty and the force of something perfectly defined, without remorse or excuse."[7]

Monroe was insecure on the first day of the shoot. To her photographer Eve Arnold she said, "How do I look?" Arnold asked her what she wanted to look like. Monroe replied, "The Botticelli Venus."[8]

Arnold was one of a number of photographers from the Magnum Agency who was given sole rights to the film. This was an unusual move by United Artists. There were nine of them in all. It was a clever move and avoided distractions for the stars. Inge Morath was another one. She would go on to feature in Miller's life in a way he could never have imagined.

Though born in Austria, she grew up in Germany. Two of her brothers had been in the army. Her uncle was a general. She spent some time working in a factory before becoming a journalist and a photographer.

She was pleased with the freedom she had. It meant she could get better "candids" of the cast. In later times this wouldn't have been possible. Today the stars often have their agents *in situ*. Everything is more contrived.[9]

Monroe wasn't pleased with the wig she'd been given for the film. It was an upswept platinum one with no bed head curls. This was practical because of the wind and the dryness of the desert. It also meant she didn't have the daily inconvenience of washing and setting it.[10]

She wasn't pleased with the fact that the film was going to be shot in black and white either. After *Some Like It Hot* she was looking forward to getting back to Technicolor. Her contract stipulated that all her Fox Films be shot in color. Billy Wilder's get-out on this score related to the fact that the thick makeup Lemmon and Curtis had to wear for their sex changes became green in color, making them look like clowns.[11]

According to Norman Mailer it suited her to have the film made in black and white. It meant she wouldn't show "every wash of bloodshot in the lost white of her eyes."[12]

"All of my important pictures have been made in color," Monroe declared.[13] This wasn't true. *Don't Bother to Knock* wasn't. It was one of her favorite films. *The Asphalt Jungle* and *All About Eve* were also shot in black and white. And, as mentioned, *Some Like It Hot*. The fact that she photographed better in color was beside the point. Huston wasn't concerned about that. The grain of the film had to mirror its tone. This was downbeat.

Huston cut the film as he shot it. His editor, George Tomasini, soundproofed a two-room suite in the Mapes. He installed a Moviola as well as work benches and a projection booth to facilitate this.

In the first scene we see Monroe with Thelma Ritter. Ritter is her friend Isabelle. Isabelle is a kindly soul, an eccentric woman who's always blaming herself for her divorce. She has a broken arm. It's one of the many things that are broken in her life. In this scene she tries to coach Roslyn through a speech she has to give in court to secure her divorce. Roslyn had difficulty remembering her lines in the scene. People who were cynical about Miller thought he wrote it to make fun of Monroe. Looked at from another point of view it's an assault on mechanical speeches, be they given by spouses who manufacture reasons why marriages failed or actors who deliver scripts without considering their deeper meanings.

Just like Roslyn failed to remember the speech her lawyer gave her so she could procure her divorce, so Monroe bridled against the words Miller gave her. She said she didn't want to live in a world where where everything was circumscribed. In the convoluted algebra of her emotions no such tidiness could be countenanced.

Strasberg, she said, told her that two and two don't necessarily make four: "Two apples and two pears make fruit salad. Two rabbits and two rabbits might make ninety rabbits."[14] This kind of thinking played havoc with her ability to do scenes quickly. "I can't remember words," she said, "I can only remember feelings."[15]

She's standing before a mirror when she talks to Ritter. Huston often uses mirrors in the film. Here it emphasizes her displacement status, "as if divorce threatens to propel her through a looking glass into a haunted world of bars and slot machines.[16]

"It's not the way it was," she says of the speech. Isabelle isn't concerned about the nuances. She just wants Roslyn to impress the judge. "You could touch him but he wasn't there," Roslyn says of her husband. Already we're seeing some of the pretentiousness that dogs Miller's script. Often in the film one is aware of the pen of a playwright rather than a screenwriter.

Guido is outside the house. He's examining her dented car – another broken thing. The dents are from men bumping into it deliberately to give themselves an excuse to start a conversation with Roslyn. Guido is there to give her an estimate on what it might be worth. He's a mechanic. She wants him to sell it for her. He's looking up at the window of the boarding house where Isabelle has been speaking to Roslyn.

Huston shot this scene the day after the previous one. Monroe hadn't arrived on the set yet. It was the first in an interminable series of absences from the star. Pumped up with sleeping pills, she found it difficult to wake up in the mornings.

*Roslyn calls down to Guido from the boarding house window in the opening scene of the movie.*

Guido calls up to her. He's yelling up to an empty window. Some spectators gathered around the set to watch him. Earlier they'd witnessed Huston telling some members of his crew to bash Rosyln's car up so the dents would be visible. Said Wallach, "They must have thought movie making was some kind of insanity – beat up a new Cadillac and then talk to an empty window.[17]

Roslyn and Isabelle go to Reno in Guido's car. Roslyn's husband Raymond (Kevin McCarthy) is waiting for her on the steps of the courthouse. It was the same building where Miller divorced Mary Slattery to marry Monroe.

Monroe had a problem crossing the road. She stopped three times and went back to the path. Huston asked her what was wrong. She said, "I forgot my motivation." Huston was nonplussed. He said, "Your motivation comes from your need to cross the street without getting hit by any of the cars." His bluntness worked. She crossed it without any problem on the next take.[18]

Huston was unimpressed with the fussiness that had come into Monroe's acting since *The Asphalt Jungle*. He saw it as threatening the very thing that made her the most loved actress in Hollywood for so long – her spontaneity.

Raymond is anxious to stop Roslyn from going ahead with the divorce. He makes a last minute plea with her to halt it but she isn't interested. "You're not there, Raymond," she tells him, "If I'm gonna be alone I want to be by myself."[19]

Once again, Monroe had to do the scene several times before she got it right. Her voice was inaudible for many of the takes. For some of them, McCarthy wore a microphone to amplify it. If he did a take well it wasn't necessarily printed but if Monroe did, it was.[20]

Where Monroe was concerned, directors followed the money. People paid to see her, not Kevin McCarthy. Tony Curtis and Jack Lemmon had similar problems during the shooting of *Some Like It Hot*. They expended great energy on takes that weren't printed. By the time Monroe got it right, they were often too exhausted to perform. Some cynics thought Monroe delayed doing her best take for that very reason. This is unlikely.

*Roslyn meeting her estranged husband (Kevin McCarthy) as they put their divorce in motion.*

McCarthy was grimly philosophical about it all. This is how he remembered it:

"We were rehearsing and she couldn't get all the lines done. This happened maybe six or seven times. My performance is going out the window. I'm really trying to do my stuff but it gets interrupted. Whatever secret I had for myself about how to play that stuff was gone. She finally was coming up the stairs toward me, and Huston is saying, 'I can't hear you, I can't hear you. Is she saying all the lines? I've got an idea. Let's run a line up Kevin's leg, get a microphone and put it under his tie. You won't be able to move, Kevin. Just stand there and do it.' And she still wasn't saying her little speeches. She came up maybe seventeen times. Huston says, 'She say them all?' And I say, 'Yeah, yeah, everything's all right.' And Huston said, 'Well, thanks, Kevin, nice working with you.'[21]

Clark Gable comes into the film now. He's saying goodbye to his ex-wife Susan (Marietta Tree) at a train station. Tree was one of Gable's former mistresses in real life.

Gable played the scene with his familiarly mischievous charm. Bosley Crowther wrote, "The old tomcat smile, the sly assurance, the aura of insincerity surrounding his goodbye to the lady – all of them are there."[22]

The meeting of Gable and Monroe is iconic. Two film legends share their first scene together in an offbeat atmosphere. They're both very naturalistic in it. Monroe was awed to be appearing with Gable. He said he was nervous with her, too. She was honored at this. It gratified her to know her idol was human.[23]

Gable has a scene with Wallach after the train goes off. Both of them were apprehensive about it in their different ways. Because Gable was such a legend, Wallach was nervous. Gable was nervous because of Wallach's Method credentials. On the previous night he'd sent a stand-in to Wallach's room to rehearse the scene. He wanted to see if Wallach was going to throw him some curve balls. He knew Wallach did exercises before his scenes. Such resources were far from where Gable was at. He dived straight into scenes and, like Spencer Tracy, tried to make sure he didn't bump into the furniture.

To their mutual relief, the scene worked fine. Huston broke the tension by giving them both a shot of Jack Daniels afterwards. Gable then shook Wallach's hand. After that, Wallach said, they were in character and able to get on with the business of the film: "Gable was Gay and I was Guido, his pal."[24]

Our attention now shifts to Rosyln. Isabelle wants her to throw her wedding ring into a river. It's a ritual for divorcing couples in Reno. "There's more gold there," she tells her, "than in the Klondike." Roslyn refuses, keeping the hope of marital happiness alive. This is unlike most of the people who end up in what Isabelle calls "the leave-it state."

They go into a bar. Roslyn says to Isabelle, "I always end up where I started." She talks about her childhood. Her parents weren't there for her. Now that her marriage has broken down she doesn't know what to do next. Isabelle says, "Teach school here."

Gay and Guido are drinking at the counter. Roslyn is taken with Gay's dog. Gay looks around. Guido comes over to her table. He introduces himself and Gay to her.

Monroe hadn't slept the night before the scene. She was about to act with the great Gable. She took Nembutals – her drug of

*The King of Hollywood and its especial Princess.*

choice – to knock her out. It was impossible to wake her the next morning. She was hours late on set.

Gable told her he didn't mind. It was worth it. He said she was beautiful and sexy. She apologized to him. He said not to worry. Sexy women were always late. The fact that he was receiving

*Eli Wallach, Thelma Ritter, Gable and Monroe exchanging life stories at Guido's house as they get to know one another.*

$50,000 overtime every week no doubt helped. He put his arms around her. She was in heaven.[25] She told him her nervousness had caused the delay.[26]

Gay tells Roslyn about his relaxed attitude to life, about how he lives for the moment. He encourages her, to seize the day. It's the only way to challenge life, to make a past that may have been cruel not matter so much.

Guido comes into the conversation. He says he has a vacant house. Roslyn and Isabelle are welcome to accompany him there with Gay.

Roslyn refuses Guido's offer of a ride to the house. She and Isabelle go to it in a rented car instead. It's located in Quail Canyon.

Once inside, Guido shows Roslyn around. Everywhere looks unfinished. This is another one of Miller's motifs in the film, as stated. Broken and incomplete things mirror the broken and incomplete lives of the characters. It's all drawn a bit too obviously for comfort.

"Everything just happened wrong," Guido tells his new friends. It's the story of his life and maybe every other character's life as well. The fact that they can remain jolly in such circumstances underlines their resilience. They dance on the graves of their pasts, bloodied but unbowed.

Nobody in the film makes plans. Too many of them have been dented in the past. "Maybe the only thing is the next thing that happens," Roslyn says. Expectations go no further than that in a world of fickleness.

Miller is already feeding elements of Monroe's life into Roslyn. A former dancer who's now in search of another dimension to her life, she says, "You started out just wantin' to dance, didn't you? But little by little it turns out that people aren't interested in how good you dance. They're gawkin' at you with somethin' entirely different on their minds." This is reminiscent of Monroe's belief that people projected onto sex symbols the lurid thoughts they were having themselves and then blamed them on their objects. She probably shared it with Miller.

Guido tells Roslyn his wife died in childbirth. It was in this very house. He had a puncture in his tire at the time. He wasn't able

*Roslyn looks affectionately at Gay while Isabelle adopts a more pensive pose in the background.*

to get her to the hospital in time to save her life because he didn't have a spare tire in his truck. "This was going to be the bedroom," he says, showing her one of the rooms. It's unfinished too. Roslyn likes it. "It's nicer this way," she says. It fits with her philosophy of incompletion.

The conversation doesn't work. It's not credible for two people who've just met. Miller has too many plot threads to get through. He's making the alliances too soon. Strangers don't usually open up to one another this early. Guido's grief over his wife doesn't work either. It's compromised by the fact that as he speaks of it he's wooing another woman.[27]

She dances with Gay. There's no electricity in the house so they can't have musical accompaniment. Then she gets a brainwave. They could use the car radio.

Guido rushes out to the car to turn it on. Everyone is in a party mood. Isabelle keeps time by beating a pan.

Guido breaks Gay and Roslyn up. "It's my turn," he says. Roslyn starts to dance with him. It's the scene Monroe told Wallach about when she met him. We hear more about grief.

*Cupid has started to fire his little arrows at Roslyn and Gay.*

The conversation still seems contrived. Roslyn has only known Guido a few hours and already she's in a decline about the death of a woman she never met.

"Didn't your wife dance?" she asks him.

"No," he says. "She had no gracefulness."

She says, "Why didn't you teach her to be graceful?"

He says, "You can't learn that."

She says, "How do you know? If you loved her you could have taught her anything."

Things become even more stilted when Roslyn says, "We're all dying, all the husbands and all the wives." Lines like this would have worked much better in the latter half of the film or when the relationships were more established. Here it comes across as too literary.

Wallach upstaged Monroe during the scene, twirling her around so that he ended up facing the camera instead of her. She was indignant and said to Strasberg, "Did you see that? Well the public's going to find my rear more interesting to look at than Eli's face anyway."[28] She exacted revenge during subsequent takes according to Wallach. She squeezed his shoulder hard during each one. When he took a shower afterwards he saw that it was black and blue.[29]

Dancing is a form of liberation for Roslyn, an escape from a world where everything is changing and everything is dying. Blotting her mind out, she obliterates tragedy.

She later dances around a tree outside the house. Her embrace of it was so erotic it caused people to see it as a code for masturbation. It's unlikely Huston intended this. Monroe was such a free spirit, any imputations were possible.

Inge Morath took some still photographs of her as she danced. She thought they captured her personality better than the film camera. Morath believed Monroe was best in still photography: "She was the animal trainer and the photographer was the beast." She tamed the camera, as it were, with her "poetry and grace."[30] Once Monroe was ready to be photographed, Morath said, "You could not photograph her badly if you tried. She had a shimmering quality like an emanation of water."[31]

*There was only one actress in Hollywood who could make tree-hugging into an erotic experience.*

Morath tried to get her when she wasn't posing. She loved doing that but Morath thought it wasn't the real Monroe. She took some shots of Miller too. He was usually removed and looking into the distance. Together, she thought they resembled Edward Hopper portraits.[32] Elliott Erwitt, another Magnum photographer on the set, had photographed the famous subway ventilation shot of Monroe. He didn't think she was especially beautiful but he accepted the fact that the camera loved her.[33]

No matter how she looked in the flesh, the camera alchemized her. Erwitt said that even though she was overweight at the time of the film she "didn't look fat in pictures. Often people who look attractive in person look like hell in pictures but she was the opposite."[34] His stills of her prove that point.

Henri Cartier-Bresson noted, "There's something extremely alert and vivid in her, an intelligence. It's her personality, it's a glance, it's something very tenuous. It disappears quickly and then appears again."[35] It was like a *trompe l'oeil* effect. Now you see it, now you

*Roslyn in the famous cherry dress as Gay cozies up to her.*

don't. Fred Guiles wrote, "She committed adultery with the camera."[36]

Huston now gives us the first romantic scene between Gay and Roslyn. After telling her she's beautiful he says, "What makes you so sad? You're the saddest girl I ever met." She replies, "No one ever said that to me before." This is a direct repeat of an exchange between Miller and Monroe during the early days of their courtship. He thought she regarded it as a compliment despite initial disappointment: "Men only wanted happy girls."[37] Rupert Allan disputed this, saying Monroe was "mortified" by the comment, that it exploited her "naked, wounded self."[38]

Wallach said Monroe burst into tears after doing the scene, that she begged Huston to stop shooting and departed the set afterwards. The episode, Wallach contended, "set a pattern for what was to come over the next weeks. Marilyn seemed to feel that the camera could detect her innermost thoughts."[39] Slowly but surely, Miller's script had begun to infiltrate her life. Where did one end and the other begin? Nobody knew for sure. He was getting ideas from her daily behavior. Mood changes that depressed both of them enriched his work. Monroe's demons became Roslyn's by proxy.

Roslyn, like Monroe, is unacademic. She's come from a dysfunctional family and feels rootless. Her desire for children and her love of animals also echo Monroe. Miller wrote the original story when he was still in love with her. The screenplay shows elements of disenchantment creeping in.

Monroe saw Roslyn as a sanitized version of herself.[40] She thought she was too passive and too given to platitudes.[41] The fact that Miller used things about her that she told him in confidence made her feel exploited. She married him so he could put her onto a different plateau but he used a mirror rather than a lamp. Miller didn't know why she was offended by such a lamp. He thought he was portraying some of her most endearing qualities. The two qualities he particularly admired in Monroe are also in Roslyn – "spontaneous joy" and quick sympathy.[42]

# Problems with Marilyn

Monroe's difficulty on *The Misfits* began even before the cameras started rolling. She expressed dissatisfaction with the costumes she was expected to wear in the film. Dorothy Jeakins designed them. Jeakins had designed the costumes for *Let's Make Love* as well. Monroe had problems with these too. Jeakins felt Paula Strasberg was part of the reason in both cases. She knew how big an influence she was on Monroe.

She wasn't confrontational even though she was entitled to be. Instead she apologized to Monroe. She even wrote a letter to C.O. Erickson, the production manager of the film, asking to be omitted from the credits. Neither did she seek money for any of the work she'd done up to this point. [1]

Huston celebrated his 54th birthday two weeks into the shoot. It was quite a night. Guests arrived from as far away as Paris. It was often said that you didn't so much attend Huston's parties as survive them. A tribe of Paiute Indians arrived from Utah and made him an honorary member. He became Long Shadow. Being a great sport for anything like this he declared, "I'm proud to be in the tribe and I intend to be one of the best damn Paiutes there is."[2] Wallach decided to use the occasion to try and sweet-talk Huston into giving him a role in the film he was planning to make about Freud. He gave him a photograph of himself dressed up as the psychologist but it didn't result in any offers from Huston.[3]

Huston was easy to work with. His non-invasive style of direction suited the Method-orientated cast. He was easygoing off the set too. He spent a lot of time in the casino losing vast amounts of money and not seeming to care. He looked like the kind of man who could toss his life away with a smile.

The relationship between Miller and Monroe got worse. Huston didn't interfere in this. He knew all about relationship conflict from his own failed marriages. The last thing he wanted was to be embroiled in anyone else's troubles.

Monroe went to bed early every night while Miller worked into the small hours on the screenplay. They never went out to dinner together. Miller travelled to the set every morning with Huston. Monroe went with Strasberg.

Neither of them was in any doubt about how problematic their marriage was before the film began. Miller said he was giving Monroe the screenplay as a gift but to her it seemed more like a poisoned chalice. He was doing it as much for his career as hers and ransacking her life for the raw material. Where did exploitation end and creativity begin?

Most couples undergoing problems have at least the hours of their work lives to be away from one another. That wasn't the case with these two. They were together most of the time. The situation was more tolerable to Miller than Monroe. He was used to putting up with her moods. Monroe was more likely to explode with cabin fever. She welcomed guests to their room for diversion. On set she snubbed Miller more often than not. Everyone saw it going on. Miller puffed on his pipe and acted as if he didn't care. He couldn't let his defenses down, couldn't let anyone see he was dying inside just as Monroe was dying on the outside.

Paul Newman used to say he kept his marriage to Joanne Woodward alive by the two of them having separate lives. That wasn't possible here. They were thrown together constantly. Monroe seemed annoyed by Miller being anywhere near her even if he was speaking to her or not. In all of the photographs taken by the nine photographers on the set of the film he cuts a lonely figure. Often he's standing alone or sitting on a canvas chair as he gazes into the middle distance. Huston needed him for the constant rewrites the screenplay demanded but one feels Monroe would have been happier if he was dispatched back to New York, leaving their ninth floor suite available to anyone she would prefer to have in it with her besides him. She took his advice on *Some Like It Hot* and *Let's Make Love* but here, with the screenplay he'd written specifically for her, she would have happily done without his revisions of it.

*Already the strain is beginning to show on Gable, seen here with a crew member, as he sweats after a scene.*

As the distance between them continued to grow, two camps formed on the set. One had Miller, Huston, Angela Allen, Frank Taylor and Ed Parone, Taylor's assistant. The other had Monroe, Reis, Strasberg, Clift, Snyder, Roberts and Flanagan.

Gable didn't belong to either camp, content to get on with the business of filming instead of the internecine squabbling. He summed up the tensions between the cast members when he said, "We don't belong in the same room together."[4]

Oblivious to the tensions, he got on with the job he was paid to do. He was pleased to be on a film set that in many ways was anathema to any of the ones he'd been on throughout most of his career. One day he opened up to Miller about his early days in Hollywood. Everything was done to a formula then. There wasn't much time for nuance. You finished a film on Friday and started another one the following week.

"It was really like a stock company," Gable said. He described arriving at a typical set: "My coach would get me out of the tuxedo and under the shower. While I was drying off he'd give me my first lines of dialogue. On the way to the studio I'd be trying to wake up and listen to him reading to me. They'd have my costume ready [when I got there] and I'd get into it. I'd go out and say 'Hi' to the director and meet whoever was playing the girl in the picture and try to figure out where the locale was supposed to be – Hawaii or Nome or Saint Louis or wherever. Then we'd have about twenty minutes to move into the shot and do it. By the end of the week you'd have a pretty good idea of what the character was. Then you'd have two more weeks till [the film] was finished. By the time you really understood anything it was over. Most of the pictures didn't have any character to speak of anyway so you sort of just made up something as you went along. Or maybe you didn't make up anything because there was nothing to make up. This one's altogether different, though."[5]

It certainly was. There was angst aplenty, and ruminations like he'd never experienced before. No wonder he was confused when Miller first showed him the script. This was revisionist, it was existential. Huston's "eastern" western wasn't so much about how the west was won as how it was lost.

The divisions in the camps intensified. If you were pro-Marilyn you were said to be anti-Arthur. If you were pro-Huston, you were anti-Paula.[6]

The question most mornings was what time Monroe would show up for work – if she showed up at all. Huston pushed back the shooting time from nine to ten, then ten to eleven, then even beyond that. "MM", as often as not, stood for "Missing" Monroe rather than her initials. As one writer put it, "Waiting for Godot was nothing compared to waiting for Marilyn."[7]

The most obvious reason for her absenteeism was her difficulty in waking up because of her addiction to sleeping pills. She herself suggested another one. "Was I punishing my father?" she wondered. "Getting even with him for all the years he kept me waiting?"[8]

Noons came and went. She found it difficult to waken from the amphetamines she'd ingested the night before. Makeup was sometimes applied while she was in bed. She was led to the shower. Then there was the long drive to the set. In the intense heat this made her even groggier.

And so the cycle began – pills to bring her up, pills to bring her down, even pills to keep her somewhere in the middle. Huston once said he saw her devour over twenty tablets in a day.[9]

The crew became enraged. Huston put up with it as Billy Wilder had on *Some Like It Hot*. When she was good she was very good. Wilder used to say that working with her was like going to the dentist – great when it was over.[10]

Wilder had many spats with her during the shooting of *Some Like It Hot*. Huston kept his anger more under wraps. Miller thought that didn't suit her, that she enjoyed the flare-ups. Maybe they even stimulated her. Maybe she fed on aggression. Maybe it confirmed her belief that much of humanity was worthless, that long-lasting relationships were impossible. Miller poured such feelings into Roslyn. At times it appeared Monroe was appearing in her autobiography.

Gable's patience with her was unwavering. He had an affection for her and was also flattered by the way she told him repeatedly

*A rare moment of relaxation for Gable and Monroe on the troubled set.*

that he'd been her idol as a child. Everyone likes praise and film stars more than most. He showed his gratitude with the kind of gracious gestures that would have been more common in his heyday than in 1960. The set was full of so-called men but it was Gable who brought a chair for her to sit on between takes. He always had that old world charm about him.

It was written into his contract that he departed the set every day at five but he was willing to bend the rules for her. There were days when she was only coming to life then.

Eve Arnold wrote about a day when she arrived on time one morning and surprised everyone. But she didn't re-appear after lunch. When the time came for her to do a scene with Clift, he'd fallen asleep and had to be woken up.[11]

Both Huston and Clift knew they had to catch this particular ball on the hop. If they didn't it might be a day or a week before she got in "the zone" again. They knew all about her antics on *Let's Make Love* and *Some Like It Hot*.

Strasberg indulged her tantrums. At times she even caused them, encouraging her to rebel against anything she saw as hierarchical behavior either in Miller or Huston. She derailed the production like a wraith hovering at the edge of it, not saying much but conveying her displeasure by looks, gestures, asides.

Huston knew she'd undermined George Cukor's authority on *Let's Make Love*. He was determined it wouldn't happen to him here. He decided on a policy of surface civility to stave off tensions. He was polite to her whenever they had occasion to speak but never allowed their exchanges go anywhere beyond that.

Miller's evaluation of her was that she didn't know any more about acting than the cleaning woman in the foyer of a theatre.[12] He thought Strasberg fed off the fact that Monroe was lonely for female company and in need of a listening ear.

Monroe's excessive reliance on her proved to be even more unnerving than her unpunctuality. She sat with her in her trailer going through the finer points of her performance the way a director would. She was impressed by the fact that she'd been a member of The Group Theatre when she was young – and, like Miller, had Communist Party affiliations. She fed into Monroe's

*Hollywood's most alluring sex symbol sits between two Hollywood hunks in the Mapes hotel but both of them seem less interested in her charms than what's on the menu.*

aspirations about where the second phase of her career might take her now that she was trying to slough off her cheesecake overtones. Strasberg encouraged her to explore the deep reserves of herself for her performance, even her breathing. Marlon Brando once said an actor should know the weight of spit in his mouth before he spoke. Monroe was fascinated by this way of thinking. Strasberg epitomized it for her.

People started making more fun of her as the shoot went on. Huston said she reminded him of a character from Greek mythology. Occasionally one of the crew would rub their hand in the sand of the desert and place it on her rump, leaving the mark for everyone to see without her being aware of it. It was cruel to do this to a woman who was unwell but her arrogance invited it.

Huston sometimes mocked her by praising her lavishly. She didn't see through this at first. He listened to her "with a seriousness so profound as to be ludicrous."[13] If he liked a scene but Strasberg didn't, Monroe would want to do it again. She wrote notes on Monroe's scripts saying things like, "You are a tree" and "You are a bird flying." After a time she started to exhaust Huston. It became like working through a translator.

Huston started to gamble more now. At this time he was having his home in St. Clerans renovated. The cost was going to be over $1 million dollars. His salary for the film wasn't anywhere near that. He thought if he got a good run of the dice he might be able to make it up.[14]

Monroe was resentful of the amount of time he spent gambling. "That's what he really likes," she said. "Not directing. I wish he'd give me as much time as the damn slot machines."[15]

Huston knew it was hit and miss with Monroe. When she was on song she could be luminescent but the pills were taking such a toll on her he was never sure when he'd get a good take. Shooting the film was like a form of gambling.

He visited her one Sunday afternoon in her suite to get some idea of what to expect from her in the weeks ahead. "She greeted me euphorically," he said, "and then went into a kind of trance. She was the worst I'd ever seen her. Her hair was a tangle. Her hands and feet were grubby. She was wearing a short nightgown which wasn't any cleaner than the rest of her. We all knew something awful was going to happen to her."[16]

Her unpunctuality became worse. After a time people became almost immune to it. They hardly knew it was happening. It was like an endemic part of her. Sometimes she even made fun of it. "I've been on a calendar," she'd say, "but I've never been on time."[17] (In actual fact she was on time. In 1956 she was on the cover of *Time* magazine.)

The shoot struggled on. There were days when she hit the marks against everyone's expectations. That was especially so in the scenes with Gable. The fact that she liked him helped enormously. If she was at ease with a co-star she was more inclined to remember her lines and not call for repeated takes – whatever about turning up on time.

Gay gets up before Roslyn the morning after their first night together. We don't see any intimacy. It wouldn't have looked right. This is more of a father-daughter relationship than a sexual one. But how has it developed so quickly?

When Gay tried to kiss her in the car after telling her she was the saddest girl he ever saw she drew away from him. Why? She wasn't interested in him "that way." Now she seems to be. This is too sudden.

He cooks breakfast for her. Before she dresses he gives her a kiss in the bed. "It was the most thrilling moment," Monroe said.

"When he kissed me I wanted it to go on and on. It was a miracle to be in his arms."[18] Was she lovesick for Montand? Depressed over Miller's coldness? The reaction seems excessive.

Her back is exposed in the shot. She's obviously slept without wearing any pajamas. She's holding a bed sheet to her front. In one of the takes it fell down. A breast slipped out. She wanted Huston to use that take but he refused. "I've seen 'em before," he said. "I've always known that girls have breasts." He claimed they bored the hell out of him: "It's the same reaction I had to a long, pointless joke."[19]

Monroe thought the nudity would make audiences sit up when the film was released. "Let's get people away from their television sets," she said. "I love to do things the censors wouldn't allow. After all, what are we here for – just to stand around and let {things] pass us by? Gradually they'll let down the censorship. Sadly, probably not in my lifetime."[20] The take wasn't used in the end. Huston thought it would shift attention away from the tenderness of the scene and onto a part of Monroe's past in films that she was trying to shed. Sometimes she seemed to be her own worst enemy.

With or without the shot, Huston felt the film was going to be a problem for the censors on a number of fronts. He'd already lost hope of procuring a seal from the Motion Picture Association. Its head Geoffrey Shurlock had been unimpressed with the sexual relationship between Gable and Monroe. He thought it was normalized by Miller's script. He was also unimpressed by terms like "hell," "damn" and "bastard" which were sprinkled throughout. It was over twenty years since Gable fell foul of the censors with his famous, "Frankly, my dear, I don't give a damn" to Vivien Leigh in *Gone with the Wind*. Similar concerns still seemed relevant.[21]

Such problems are far from the minds of Gay and Roslyn as they have their breakfast. They chat amicably. It's a naturalistic moment in the film that's free from Miller's heaviness elsewhere.

Huston closes his camera in on Monroe as she leans over the table. She says to Gable, "You like me, hunh?" It's a simple line well delivered.

As they continue chatting we learn that Gay's daughter is a size 12. It's Roslyn's size too. A patriarchal connection is established.

*Gable looks happy here but a man of his age shouldn't have been carrying cement blocks – like the one on which he's resting his foot – to make a step for himself and Roslyn at Guido's house.*

Gay opens up about his wife's infidelity. Roslyn says, "Everything keeps changing." It's not your usual breakfast conversation. Then comes the howler. He says, "I wouldn't know how to say goodbye to you." He's hardly said hello.

If Roslyn is Monroe, Gable is Miller. The age disparity between them is much greater of course but Gay's marital status, his residence in Reno, his two children from a previous marriage and the fact of his being cuckolded by his wife – the memory of Montand rankled with Miller as he wrote the screenplay – all reflect his situation.

Huston was so impressed with the way Monroe did the scene that he embraced her. Any Monroe scene that was expedited quickly was a joy. The embrace may have been part relief.

It was captured on camera. When Monroe saw it she asked the photographer to keep it. "I want to have it to show around," she said, "when he begins saying mean things about me."[22] The remark suggests something of a siege mentality. Huston hadn't said any mean things yet but he may have conveyed them by his attitude. She found him to be patronizing as time went on. She thought it could have been due to the fact of Miller complaining to him about her. "That's why he treats me like an idiot," she said, "with his 'Dear this' and 'Dear that.'"[23] This was an over-reaction. Huston spoke to most women that way. It was part of his personality.

*A riding expedition for the new lovers.*

Gable and Monroe go horse riding now. There's a shot of Monroe's bottom which was regarded as voyeuristic. It bops up and down on the saddle. Afterwards they have a swim. Huston delayed the scene because of Monroe's increasing weight. She was oblivious to this. She'd been looking forward to showing off her skin-colored bikini for the scene but her display didn't go down well. None of the crew was really interested. They were too fed up with her unpunctuality and her disruptiveness to be able to enjoy her "sexy act."[24] Their apathy was a blow to her pride. When Angela Allen asked them if they thought Monroe was the ultimate standard of feminine beauty, they shouted out "No!" in unison.[25] Allen and Monroe hadn't liked one another from the start of the film. Monroe suspected Allen of having an affair with Miller at one point.

Eve Arnold thought Monroe was in denial about her increased weight. "She'd lost all the contours of a young woman," she said.[26] She was still very attractive but she could have done with being a bit more subdued in this scene.

The subsequent scenes between Gay and Roslyn don't work any better as their relationship takes off. We see them engaging in all sorts of activities like making a step outside the front door. Monroe skips up and down on this like a child, to Gable's delight.

Everything is still happening too fast – from horse riding to swimming to Gay doing tasks for Roslyn around the house and in the garden. They've gone from being total strangers to acting like husband and wife. This might have worked better for a couple closer in age. One feels Miller is forcing the issue, especially in view of Roslyn's initial rebuff of him. The lines he's called on to say to her don't sound like the way real people talk to one another. They're too literary.

They sound more realistic when they're talking about ordinary things, like garden pests.

When jackrabbits threaten his vegetables, Gay wants to kill them. Roslyn pleads with him not to. Their encounter prefigures the penultimate scene with the mustangs.

Guido and Isabelle arrive at the house. Guido sees there are some photographs from Roslyn's past inside the door of a locker. "Gay just put them there for a joke," she says. This is a barbed line.

*Gay and Roslyn put down some roots together – literally.*

Monroe spoke it from the heart. She saw the photographs as a trivialization of her own past rather than Roslyn's.

Guido starts to talk about his past. He says he wanted to be a doctor. This is fine but it segues into him saying he wouldn't be able to re-design his house if he hadn't met Roslyn. How can he say this when he hardly knows her?

He tells her she has "the gift of life." It sounds like excessive praise. What we're hearing is Miller's feelings about the young Monroe. All Roslyn has done so far is dance around a tree. People are continually flattering her in the film, making huge claims about her charisma. Gay says her smile is like the sun coming up. These are arresting images but the bottom line is that she's a deeply troubled soul. The lines have been written by Miller to try and placate Monroe. He was trying to deflect rumors that the marriage was on the rocks. The Monroe he's speaking about has been plucked from the past, from when he first knew her. The woman who was on set with him was a different being. If she truly had the gift of life she wouldn't have wanted to end it. By now she'd made many suicide attempts.

The conversation turns to mustanging. They need another man. They know a rodeo rider called Perce.

The stage is set for the entrance of Montgomery Clift.

*The patriarch and his dreamy daughter figure.*

# Perce

After Clift arrived in Reno to start the film he was sent off to Idaho to learn how to handle wild horses. This made sense as he doesn't feature in any of the early scenes.

He prepared for the role by riding up to six hours a day in the desert with Dick Pascoe, his stunt double. He accompanied Pascoe to a rodeo one day in the town of Potacello to get the feel of what it was like to be in the enclosures where the cowboys sat on bucking bulls. At one point he bent over a chute to help a cowboy climb onto the back of a Brahma bull and got cut on the nose by the bull's horns. Miller used this to give him an injury in the film.

In his first scene we see him on the phone to his mother. She's a woman he has a strong attachment to. He tells her he's recovering from a rodeo accident. He says his face is so badly scarred she'll probably have difficulty recognizing him. Gay, Roslyn and Guido look at him from their car as he's speaking.

Read between the lines and we get: He's a gay man (mother affinity) who's been injured in a car accident. Miller is continuing to plunder his stars' lives for material.

Monty was nervous about the phone booth scene, especially since he was being watched by so many actors he revered. For him it was like an audition in front of "the gods and goddesses of the performing arts."[1]

Huston thought he performed it perfectly. Clift wanted to do it again to improve on the scene but Huston said no, that they had to press on.

Writer Robert Thom accused Miller of being "ghoulish and cold-blooded" to have written a scene where Clift is so badly scarred considering his car accident in real life took so much out of him. Miller defended himself by saying he'd written *The Misfits* story long before Clift signed up for the part.[2]

*Clift mimics Marilyn in a rare camp moment for him. The other men in the cast are more intent on establishing their macho credentials.*

This was true but he added to it afterwards. Clift had the right to object if he wished. If he had, Miller would have changed it. The fact that he didn't object suggested he didn't mind. This is surprising. Clift steered conversations away from the accident in his private life and also kept in the closet about his sexual orientation. He refused parts that might have given innuendoes as to his sexuality, like for instance a role in *Sunset Boulevard* where he would have been in a relationship with a much older woman. This was often seen as a gay code. This never became an issue with man's

*Gay giving Roslyn some encouragement for her paddlebatting. He wouldn't have got away with this in a later era.*

man William Holden taking on the role of Joe Gillis. It might have been with Clift. Why was he changing his attitude now? Probably because he liked the part so much.

Clift surprised everyone by his upbeat mood on the set. His car accident had devastated him but it also freed him from the "boy next door" status he had among some viewers. Good looks meant he couldn't always get inside a character in the way he wanted. He didn't have that problem now. They weren't a distraction. "I have to find the real me outside my looks," he said. His fans had always been obsessed with his appearance. "And so was I."[3]

Clift brought a bruised dignity to the role of Perce. Huston saw him as a pillar of the production despite his small role. Maybe its brevity helped. He always found it difficult to remember lines. Most Method actors liked to improvise them. That worked better with some directors than others. Clift had a difficult time with Alfred Hitchcock in *I Confess*. Hitchcock's penchant for nailing scenes down like trigonometrical formulas flew in the face of his need for experimentation. Huston was more flexible in that regard. He didn't mind trying a scene a number of ways to find which one worked best. It was surprising he didn't ask Clift to do the first scene again when he said he wanted to.

Perce now sits into the car with Roslyn, Gay and Guido. There's an instant empathy between them. They may be misfits from society's point of view but they aren't to one another. Misfits slot into their own enclaves.

Perce has hardly entered the film before he's asking Gay to get him some whiskey. Here again Miller is tapping into something he knows about Clift rather than Perce.

His merging of life and art continues when they go into a bar. Roslyn starts playing with a paddle bat. This had happened off set. Miller was entranced watching Monroe do it so he wrote it into the scene.

People start placing bets on how many times she can bounce the ball off the bat. Miller was aware of how much people loved to gamble in Nevada. They didn't need a casino to do it. The fact that Nevada was legal helped. This wasn't the case in most other states.

Estelle Winwood comes into this scene. She plays a woman soliciting funds to erect a fence in the town's graveyard. Roslyn

*Estelle Winwood, left, asks Roslyn for a contribution to a fence she's hoping to have built in the town's graveyard. Money means nothing to Roslyn but Gay is reluctant for her to part with what's in the hat.*

gives her a lot of the money she's won from the gambling. We can see Miller doing everything he can to display Monroe's kind heart. Gay has to stop her eventually.

Monroe was in high form during the scene. As one point she put Winwood's wig on. A confused extra asked her if she was Marilyn Monroe. "No," she replied, "I'm Mitzi Gaynor."[4]

Her periods of elation were usually followed by ones of exhaustion. So it proved here. Her energy level dipped after the scene. She was late – or absent – in later ones. People sat in cars waiting for her. They were grateful to have air conditioning in their vehicles to deaden the heat of the sun. She was massaged into drowsiness by Roberts at night and into wakefulness by him in the mornings. Nembutal, Doriden, Luminal and Seconal were administered in different dosages.[5]

Huston told Miller he needed to do something about her. Miller said he wasn't able to. Huston accepted this. "I can't function before noon," she said, "so what's the point of being on the set before then?"[6]

It seemed to conduce to some sort of logic. Frank Taylor's son Curtice watched the absurdity unfold. It was, he said, "like working with a hangover."[7]

People watched her with a mixture of shock and awe. When would they witness the next explosion of anger – or need? When would she be brilliant? When would she crumble?

Her moods were like clouds moving across the sun. She cut Wallach dead one day for no reason. Another day she compared him to Miller: "Oh, you Jewish men!"[8]

We now get the rodeo scene. It was filmed in Dayton, a ghost town south of Virginia City. Clift rides a bucking horse. When Clift and Gable were being driven through the rodeo parade, Clift kept punching Gable playfully in the arm. Gable had arthritis and roared at him to stop. Clift was so sensitive he burst into tears because of Gable's anger. A bewildered Gable said, "What in fuck is the world coming to?"[9]

Clift had an actual accident at the rodeo. A horse throws him onto the side of a wooden chute. His shirt is nearly ripped from his back. Huston used the incident for Perce.[10]

*Roslyn is visibly distressed at Perce's rodeo injury. Guido tries to comfort her as he receives attention.*

Roslyn becomes hysterical when she witnesses him being injured. She offers him money so he won't have to ride again. Her reaction is excessive. It's like her reaction to the fact that Guido's wife died. At least this time her fretting is about a person she actually knows. But how long does she know him? Miller is microscoping lives into days. One might argue that all art does this. One might also argue that the character of Roslyn is beautifully drawn. Thinking about her like this gives the scene some credibility.

She expresses her concern to Gay about the fact that Perce could die. He replies, "Nothing can live unless something else dies." This is bad writing. What he needed to say was something ordinary like, "Don't worry. He'll be fine." That's how people speak when they're in the middle of a crisis. Philosophical speculations are made in studies, in hospitals, in churches, at funerals. We don't expect to hear them when someone is lying on the ground at a rodeo show and nobody is quite sure if they're seriously injured or not.

# Meltdown

Everyone went to a dry area called Pyramid Lake for the final scenes. It was a location used for science fiction films, an Indian reservation that looked exactly the way it was "when God made the world."[1]

The land was flat and boring. The only trees visible were those erected by the prop men. It was a sixty mile drive for the cast. They made their way there every day at 9 a.m., their cars traveling at a safe distance from one another so the drivers wouldn't be blinded by the alkali dust thrown up from the desert sand.

Everyone was at the end of their tether. They wanted things to be wrapped up. There was too much tension, too much misery. Huston realized he'd bitten off much more than he could chew. One writer described him as being stranded in a minefield among a crew of manic depressives.[2]

They searched inside themselves for the energy to continue with a project that seemed to be coming apart at the seams. Monroe's delays, Huston's preoccupation with gambling and the increasing divisions between the various factions – everything seemed worse because of the heat and the draining journey to a set that looked as lost as the actors inhabiting it.

"Tempers sizzled," wrote Susan Strasberg. "The hours drained away like the sands in an hourglass. The shoot had become the St. Valentine's Day Massacre."[3]

By now things had collapsed completely between Monroe and Miller. She'd even started to blame him for her problems with Billy Wilder on *Some Like It Hot*.[4] Wallach said he often heard them arguing in their room.

They argued so much there were complaints from the occupants of the rooms around them. Monroe told Miller that Montand was going to leave Signoret for her. She told him he was cold, that he was more attached to his mother than he was to her. She blamed him for getting rid of Milton Greene, a man she now realized was one of the few people who hadn't exploited her.[5]

Huston hated the way Monroe treated Miller. She insulted him in front of others. He'd act like he didn't care: "He would pretend he wasn't listening." Her hangers-on carried on the humiliation: "I think they hoped to demonstrate their loyalty to Marilyn by being impertinent to Arthur. On these occasions Arthur never changed expression."[6]

One day Huston saw Miller looking forlorn as he stood in the middle of a road after shooting had finished. Monroe's car came towards him and then sped off without him. Some accounts of this incident have her actually slamming the door on him. This was probably an exaggeration but the two camps had become increasingly more polarized by now. The "neutrals," like Wallach, felt sorry for Miller. "He looked hollow-eyed and lost," Wallach said. "Give him a beard and he could pass for Abraham Lincoln."[7] The first time Monroe met him, interestingly, she told him he looked like Lincoln. This was a point noted by Norman Mailer in his "alibiography" of her, *Of Women and Their Elegance*.[8]

The sun beat down mercilessly. Monroe rehearsed lines with Strasberg in her limousine. Huston seemed removed from the production, spending more and more time in the casino. He stayed

there all night sometimes and fell asleep in his director's chair the next morning. He might even forget what scene he was supposed to shoot. "Chaos was on us all," said Miller.[9]

He was shell shocked from everything that had happened in the few short months since shooting began. A project that promised so much now looked to be about to deliver very little. This despite all his efforts. Maybe he put too much into it. There were days when it was the only thing on his mind, when it became a bigger world to him than his plays, his marriage, his life. He watched a group of girls playing tennis when he was out walking one night and was amazed to see that there were still people in the world who could do something as simple as hitting a ball back and forth across a net. He found it "miraculous." Back at the hotel he watched Huston shoot craps with a glass of scotch in his hand, "his bush jacket as crisply pressed as if he'd put it on ten minutes before." He was losing $25,000. Miller went to bed. When he came down the next morning at seven a.m. Huston was still at the table. He'd won back the money and was now trying to win some more.[10]

Angela Allen was feeling the pressure too. Monroe still thought she was having an affair with Miller. One day a friend of hers said, "Are you enjoying it?" She threatened to quit the film. "I try to be sweet, calm and gentle," she said, "but it never lasts long."[11]

Monroe went into the makeup man's room one night. She told him she wanted to sleep there to get away from Miller. The makeup man conveyed the message to Miller. He said he'd move out of the suite they shared if she wanted. The move was long overdue. They were getting ready to tear one another apart. Why hadn't he done it before? When he was leaving, all he took with him was his typewriter. Strasberg moved into the suite with Monroe after he was gone. They later went to the Holiday Inn together.

Huston's sympathies still lay with Miller. He did his best to make the marriage work, he said, and got nothing but rudeness back from Monroe. Like Wallach he'd witnessed the incident in the desert where she'd left him in the middle of the road as her car zoomed towards Reno. Huston had to drive Miller back to the hotel that day. "There were no other cars," he said. "It was sheer malice, vindictiveness."[12]

The film neared completion. As if it wasn't enough for the cast and crew to be snapping, the world of nature did now as well. In the middle of August two forest fires raged unchecked over 35,000 acres of timberland. Firefighters did their best to hold them back but it was a losing battle. The flames cut Reno's power lines. Arson was suspected but never proved.

The only lights visible in the town were those in the big casinos. Huston hauled in the film company's diesel generator to illuminate the one in the Mapes. He also had a cable run to the room Miller was now staying in. He felt as privileged as the casinos. People were bewildered looking up at the single light burning several feet above them every night. Miller was bewildered too. He couldn't understand how they'd done it. "Movie crews love the impossible," he said. "It makes them feel real."[13]

The failure of the electrical supply resulted in a different kind of problem when one of the elevators became stuck between two floors. The man operating it ended up being trapped inside. Huston felt sorry for him. He arranged to have some whiskey delivered to him through a small aperture in the door. The man guzzled away to his heart's content. When the power came back and the doors opened, he fell out onto the floor. He was sozzled. Huston was amused. A boozer himself, he felt for him.

The crew had a party on the ninth floor of the Mapes soon afterwards. Ralph Roberts and Agnes Flanagan were drinking champagne by candlelight. Monroe thought they looked romantic. There were lots of other people there as well – Susan Strasberg, May Reis, Whitey Snyder and Rupert Allan. They were all huddled into the wardrobe department. Monroe sat on a trunk. At one stage she grabbed a wig that was lying around, doing an imitation of Mitzi Gaynor just like she had after the paddle bat scene of the film in the bar. Without mentioning Miller's name she sang "I'm Gonna Wash That Man Right Outta My Hair." She didn't need to.[14]

Miller didn't attend the party. Tiredness overcame him. He decided to have a drink in his room instead. At one point of the night Monroe needed some ice. She asked Roberts to get it for her from the man she now referred to as "Grouchy Grumps."

*Miller with the script of the film in his hand, but Marilyn doesn't seem to want it. "I wrote it as a gift to her," he said, "but I left the set without her."*

When he came back with it she asked him if he'd spoken to him. Roberts said he hadn't, that he was just lying on the sofa. Monroe said he'd probably stay like that for the rest of the night in between bursts of writing and drinking: "From the desk to the sofa and back again," she chided, adding as she dropped one of the ice cubes into her glass, "Klunk!"[15]

She started talking to Allan. They gazed out over the Truckee River. Allan ruminated about the life cycle of fish, how so many of them went upriver at the end of their lives "to be eaten by other fish or by the raccoons." Monroe said she could understand something not resisting death. She told him of an occasion when she'd contemplated taking her life in New York. She'd climbed out onto the ledge of her thirteenth-floor apartment in her nightgown and looked down at the street below. "I saw a woman in a brown tweed suit," she said, "and I thought if I jumped I would do her in too. I waited out there for about five or ten minutes but she didn't move. I got cold so I climbed back in. But I would've done it."[16]

Allen told her he too had felt suicidal at times. He suggested they make a pact. If either of them ever thought of it again they would phone the other and they'd talk them out of it. Their code word would be "Truckee River." Monroe was said to have made similar pacts with Norman Rosten and Lee Strasberg.[17]

Another version of this anecdote has her confiding such thoughts to Ralph Roberts. In this version she recognized the woman. She was tempted to jump, she's alleged to have told Roberts, because she read somewhere that people who fall from heights lose consciousness before they hit the ground.[18]

She woke up the next morning with a massive hangover. "I feel like I drank all the gin in the world last night," she said.[19] She became depressed in the days following. It was as if the night created a kind of death wish in her. She attempted suicide one night. It may have been a call for help. Her stomach was pumped and she rallied.

Miller felt helpless. "I was almost completely out of her life now," he said.[20] Her speech was incoherent and her walk unsteady. She hardly slept at all. When she did she had nightmares. Her skin broke out in rashes.

Lee Strasberg visited the set. He was more concerned about how his wife was being treated than about Monroe. Miller was flummoxed as he talked to him. He didn't seem to know about Monroe's problem. "Paula?" he thought. Was this really about Paula rather than Marilyn? His get-up was almost as ridiculous as hers. He wore a cowboy suit with braided pockets. "The situation has become impossible," he told Miller. Miller agreed but he said there was nothing he could do about it: "It's my script, not my picture."[21]

She overdosed on August 26. Miller knew the situation was critical. Her throat diaphragm was paralyzed. He rang a medical

*Marilyn looks ready for 'action' – for once!*

clinic and they sent an ambulance. The emergency team revived her despite all the pills she'd swallowed.

She'd been on every kind of pill for years - "pills to make her sleep, pills to wake her, pills to slow her up when she was too stimulated, pills to tone her down, pills to overcome pills."[22] By now she was on upwards of 300 milligrammes of Nembutal a night. The standard dose is 100 milligrammes. Immunity sets in after that.

A diet of sleeping pills, as everyone knows, eventually catches up on people. They need more and more of them. Monroe put so much intensity into life, she couldn't turn her mind off like a light switch at the end of a day. And she couldn't turn it on at the beginning of one. And so it went on, the cycle of uppers and downers. She'd been practicing it since the forties in some shape or form.

A doctor gave her a shot of Amytal. When Miller went in to see her she screamed at him. By now the very sight of him worked her up. He was amazed she had the energy to scream after receiving such a powerful injection. She reminded him of "a flower of iron." She wanted to ride "the next wave thundering towards the shore." He felt useless to her, "a bag of nails thrown in her face." He felt sad that they could never live a normal life again, "an ordinary decom-pressed life down on the plain, far away from this rarefied peak where there was no air."[23]

There was no way she could continue filming. The set was closed down. It was the second time in Huston's career that he'd had to do so. The other one was when Audrey Hepburn broke her back while making *The Unforgiven*.

His gambling addiction was totally out of control by now. One night he was reputed to have lost $16,000. His total losses since arriving in Reno were $50,000. This was significantly more than the production company allowed as credit. Wallach believed he didn't care if he won or lost. He was amazed at how he could be at the craps table all night and still turn up for work the next morning needing nothing more than a coffee to adrenalize him.

One of Huston's biographers said he was deeply upset about his losses, saying they were "almost as much as I'm getting for the whole damn picture."[24] Another author suggested he ran up such a debt he was prohibited from leaving Reno by gangsters until he settled it.[25] Lawrence Grobel claimed Huston went to San Fran-cisco at this time to try and procure an advance for his forthcoming film, *Freud*, to pay his debt.[26] Donald Spoto thought he was so depressed about his financial situation that he closed down the set to save on salaries, using Monroe as a scapegoat. Barbara Leaming discounted Spoto's theory entirely. The reason Huston shut down the set, she argued, was to help Monroe rather than to demonize her. He was aware that if she failed to complete the film she'd be uninsurable on future ones.[27]

The story pedaled to the press was that she was suffering from exhaustion. It was a familiar euphemism for stars who'd burned themselves out on barbiturates.

Monroe was flown to the Westside Hospital in Los Angeles for treatment. She was put under the care of Ralph Greenson and another psychiatrist, Hyman Engelberg. Miller was asked if he knew why she'd overdosed. He said he didn't, that it came from "nowhere." Monroe told Greenson that "nowhere" was the place where Miller's indifference resided.[28]

Her condition stabilized over the next few days. Once again she'd survived. But how many more times could she skate this close to the wind?

Gable flew to Encino for the break. Clift went to New York. Wallach's wife and children had just arrived in Reno so he decided to stay with them. Taylor and his wife also stayed in Reno. Huston spent the week viewing the rushes with George Tomasini.

All of the Strasbergs went to see her in hospital. Susan was particularly shocked at what she saw: "She was a ghost of herself. She lay helpless, like an overgrown child. It was as if someone had drained her life force."[29]

Huston asked Greenson if he thought she was capable of finishing the film. He knew she was on Demerol and Nembutal. Greenson reduced her Nembutal intake. Huston afterwards went to Hollywood for a conference. Monroe got further tablets from a Reno doctor unbeknownst to Greenson after she was discharged from the hospital.

On the way back to the set she called to see Joe DiMaggio in San Francisco. She told him she was going to divorce Miller as soon as *The Misfits* wrapped. DiMaggio began to think he could re-kindle his relationship with her.

She returned to the set on September 6. A large number of fans turned out to welcome her at the airport. There were messages saying, "Welcome Home, Marilyn," and "Get Well. *The Misfits* Needs You."

Even though Greenson reduced her Nembutal intake, she was still on various medications so she wasn't, as it were, "clean." She was on Demerol and another tranquillizer and in withdrawal from the Nembutal so she was feeling groggy when she faced the cameras again. She was, in the words of one writer, "immobilized" for five days after her return.[31]

Miller danced with her in a bar after her first day back. He was in unusually spirited form. His head was thrown back and his arms sticking out like semaphores. He was trying to tell Clift how to do a polka. It was the scene after the rodeo and everyone was pumped up. Monroe went for a walk with him that evening, no doubt impressed by his rare bout of extroversion.

*'The eyes have it.' Marilyn often seemed miles away from what was happening in the film. Who was she thinking about here – Yves Montand? Joe DiMaggio? It was hardly Arthur Miller.*

Roberts said her personality changed after she came back. She put black curtains over the windows of her room to shut out the light, thereby creating a womb – or tomb – for herself. Roberts said she was like a caged animal, afraid of both day and night.[32]

She'd lost weight in the hospital. This worked to her advantage in the film, making her look more attractive in the next scenes she shot. She was in better form than anyone had seen her for a long time. Maybe they'd get the film finished after all.

The following scene had Wallach getting drunk with Gable while Monroe and Clift dance behind them at a jukebox. Clift gets dizzy from his injury so she takes him outside.

Huston felt Wallach overdid his drunkenness. He didn't say this directly to him. Instead he said, "Do you know the drunkest I ever was in my life?" Wallach said he didn't. Huston said, "Yesterday."[33]

Wallach was confused. The previous day was Labor Day. Huston hadn't looked drunk. In fact he'd entered a camel race and won it. Wallach got the point. Drunk people didn't always act drunk. A good drunk scene was when you tried to act soberer than you were. Wallach did the scene better on the next take. "A drunk tries to be sober," he remarked.[34] Once again, Huston's non-invasive style of direction worked.

*Roslyn comforts Perce after his head injury in the best scene in the film.*

We now get an excellent scene between Perce and Roslyn. It lasts five minutes. He tells her he lost his ranch and turned to bronco riding to make ends meet. Huston thought the scene would be problematic because of Monroe's moods and Clift's history but it only took three takes. They both blew one each. Instead of becoming frustrated about this they collapsed laughing. Monroe praised Clift for his acting and he was touched. He savored the praise "like a parched leaf savors a rainshower."[35]

"How come you got so much trust in your eyes?" he says at one stage. "It's like you was just born." He's tapping into the innocence for which Monroe was noted when first she graced a cinema screen, the innocence Miller fell in love with. Was it still there? Maybe it was in Roslyn more than Monroe. Her character was all he had to cling on to as the marriage drifted away from him.

Roslyn is like a mother to Perce in this scene. He talks about losing everything when his father died and his mother re-married. She says, "Maybe all we got is the next thing. Maybe we're not supposed to remember other people's promises." Here the literary lines work. This is because of the fine acting of both Clift and Monroe.

*Nobody bonded better on the set of the film than Clift and Monroe.*

They're sold into the scene. Perce says, "I think I love you." Roslyn replies, "You don't know me." At last Miller has had the good sense to undercut the big line. We needed to hear "You don't know me" long before now. We needed to hear it when Guido was talking about his dead wife and when Gay was talking about his unfaithful one. But better late than never.

This is one of the best scenes in the film. It's played to a backdrop of beer cans and junk automobiles. The two characters are diamonds in the rough. Huston saw it as a love scene.[36] Flies buzzed around them as they shot it. There were bad smells as well, and very bright lights, but they nailed it.

Roslyn cradles the injured Perce just as Elizabeth Taylor cradled Clift after the horrific accident that destroyed both his life and career. It's one of the most tender scenes in the film. Both of them gave it everything, even going so far as to ban a still photographer from the set while it was being shot so he wouldn't disrupt their concentration by the clicking of his camera.[37]

The scene was shot from a worm's eye view, the camera crew digging a hole for themselves to allow them to shoot up into the faces of Clift and Monroe. It was a "day for night" scene. Russell Metty covered the shooting area with a sheet of black tarpaulin to block the rays of the sun. Another member of the crew stood by with a can of insect spray to try and keep the flies away.

Perce is like Roslyn's gay friend just like Clift was Monroe's in real life. Though he engages in macho pursuits in the film, he seems more himself in scenes like this where he's being held by her, when he can speak intimately to her and draw her out of herself. Both of them run from the main business of the film to chill out with one another like babes in the wood. "I don't like the way they grind up women out here," he tells her. Neither does she. They confide in one another away from the action like two children seeking the kind of solace that's unavailable to them in the outside world. This is also the way it was for them in real life. Monroe said of Clift, "I look at him and see the brother I never had. I feel braver and more protective."[38]

For Clift, playing a scene with Monroe was "like an escalator. She went over the fringe. You'd do something and she'd catch it and it would go like that, just right up."[39]

He said of her, "She's the most gifted actress on the American screen. Here's real proof of how I feel about her. I'm jealous, even if I'm a man, when I watch what she does. She's so good I hate her!"[40]

He didn't see her as a sex symbol. She was more of a maternal figure to him. When he looked into her eyes, he said, it "sparked everything.[41] She brought out his vulnerability. This was his best quality. "The problem of acting," he said once, "is how to be vulnerable and thin-skinned and yet survive."[42] Monroe helped him survive. Frank Taylor said they were like "psychic twins." They recognized disaster and laughed about it.[43]

Another thing they shared in common was a dependence on Nembutal. One day during a break in filming Clift told Monroe that if she pricked a capsule and poured its contents directly into a glass of water it took effect much faster. It wasn't long before she started doing this.[44]

They talked about pills as much as about the film. Said Monroe, "We try to figure out for each other what to take to fall asleep. He can't sleep either. Monty's just like me."[45]

Clift's insomnia was so bad he had his bed shipped from New York to the Mapes along with thick black curtains for the windows. Even so, he often stayed awake until dawn.[46] Edward Parrone remarked, "Monty and Marilyn were both nervous people but Marilyn's nervousness was very different from his." Clift's biographer said, "Hers was an urgent, primitive nervousness based largely on fear. Monty's was associated with tension."[47]

Gable comes out looking for them at the end of the scene. He's seen his children and wants them to as well. They follow him out

*Gay puts a protective arm around Roslyn as Guido hovers in the background.*

to the street but when they got there the children have disappeared. He becomes distraught. He's drunk as well. He climbs onto a car and falls off it. Gable was applauded by the crew for his acting but he overcooked it. It's the kind of portrayal of drunkenness Huston dissuaded in Wallach. Henry Hart wrote in *Films in Review* that the scene was "improperly written, shot and edited."[48]

Gable wasn't interested in the nuances of Clift and Monroe. If this was what Method acting did, he thought, he could happily do without it. Give him Errol Flynn with his sabre-rattling any day of the week. He wondered if they'd finish the film. He knew Clift was getting some help in his acting from whatever substances he was ingesting. The wild look he had in his eyes, he thought, could only have come from morphine or booze.

*An inebriated Gay leaves the bar with Roslyn. He's anxious to see his children, who've recently been in Reno, but they've already gone.*

Monroe always looked out for Clift. When his jeans sagged, she told the makeup people to moisten them so they became tight. Though the overt romantic relationship in the film is between Gable and Monroe, the one between Clift and Monroe is in some ways deeper. This despite the fact that they never became sexual with one another. Clift patted Monroe's bottom on the set one day and she was amused. At other times she tantalized him with her body, rubbing her nipples across his nose. It was said that she was "determined to get him into bed for the hell of it" if nothing else. Clift tried to make love to her once but they were both too drunk at the time for anything to happen. Instead they just "fooled around."[49]

# Last Scenes

Winter hinted. Snow appeared on the Sierras. The wind got stronger on Pyramid Lake, blowing dust across the plains. People found it difficult to speak, even to breathe. Huston's bronchitis got at him. Gable's voice became hoarse. Filming was stopped to allow everyone to come to terms with the conditions. For once it wasn't Monroe who was responsible.

Wallach was the victim of a practical joke one day. It was when the motor of his plane sprung a leak. A crew member was supposed to spray him with a small amount of oil to indicate this. Bearing in mind his Method orientation he doused his whole face with it. Another crew member then shouted out, "Get him to sing '*Mammy*.'" Laughter erupted. Wallach was furious. He fixed the man with a malevolent leer and stared him down. After that the laughter stopped.[1]

Miller and Monroe continued to drift apart. Morath took a photograph of them that captures how bad things were. It's amazing that she got it as it was taken in their suite. She's looking out the window. He's standing apart from her with a cigarette in his mouth and his hands in his pockets. A picture is worth a thousand words. Nowhere was this precept more applicable than here.

The film was reaching its finale to the relief of all concerned. As one writer put it, the cast was like a Swiss Family Robinson that had been through too much together. All they wanted now was to separate and go home.[2]

We now get a scene around a campfire in the best tradition of westerns – even "eastern" ones. Roslyn is about to become educated into the cruel ways of her mustanger heroes. She's like a child in her belief that they won't kill the horses for profit.

When Gay tells her they're going to be sold for pet food he says, "I thought you knew." But how could she? It was the farthest thing

*Roslyn showing her neediness to Gay once again.*

from her mind. Her devastation at the disclosure pushes the film towards its climax.

This occurs after Guido hunts the horses out of the mountains towards the lake from his plane. Real life wrangler Bill Jones recalled procuring genuine wild ones for the film. "We got 'em right here off the mountains," he said, "Got one mustang that's a mean sonuvabitch. He stands gentle and then lets you have it with both feet. Fast as lightening he is. He'll come right at you. Mr.

Huston needed some Brahmas and some steers for the roping and bull-dogging scenes and he wanted 'em rough. Well, we brought in the roughest there is in the US and he looked real pleased."[3] Wanting them "rough" was something he would be criticized for after the film wrapped.

The scenes of lassoing the horses and tying them down with tires saved the film from an insinuation that it was too wordy and lacked action. Both Gable and Clift justified their status as mustangers here. Gable had his hands lacerated by a bucking mare. He got dragged by one too, at least ostensibly. In reality it was a truck traveling at 35 miles an hour for 400 feet.

A representative of the ASPCA stood by to ensure there was no abuse of the horses in the scene but as James Goode pointed out, there was nobody present to ensure the *actors* weren't being abused.[4] The Humane Society insisted on a trained roper being used for the scene. A man called Jim Palen was employed for this purpose. The fact that he sustained injuries in it was indicative of how graphic Huston insisted it be.

Gable had pads to protect him from bruises and burns. He wore gloves and a corset as well but it was still cruel of Huston to have a man of his age called upon to do a scene like this. Huston said a stand-in did most of the stunts.[5] But it wasn't a stand-in who was dragged by the truck, or who was seen in close-up lassoing the horses. Gable's bravado came into play as well. He wanted to be seen as the virile hero Miller created.[6]

He'd shown similar bravado when he built the concrete step with Monroe shortly after they set up house together in Quail Canyon. His friend Ernie Dunlevie recalled, "They must have shot that scene twelve to fifteen times. And it wasn't a fake block.[7]

Gable wasn't as able for the stunts as he thought he'd be. By the time they were over he was, as one writer put it, "panting like a broken down old fire engine."[8]

The crash diet he'd been put on for the duration of the film made him tire quickly.[9] Donald Spoto thought Huston was oblivious to the danger of him being trampled by the horses.[10] For some of the scenes he wasn't wearing the gloves. Clift also had his hands lacerated trying to hold down a bucking mare. He refused to wear

*Gable looks intent on lassoing the mustangs but at sixty it wasn't too wise to be still thinking of himself as an action hero*

gloves. At one stage Wallach said to him, "Look at your hands. Stop being a Christ figure."[11] There sometimes seemed to be an element of masochism in Clift's action sequences.

Kay tended Gable's cuts and burns every night at their home. She begged him to stop doing scenes like this but he wouldn't listen. He said to her, "I thought it would be easy. The horses were so tired I figured they wouldn't give me any trouble. What surprised me is that no one gave a damn if I got killed or not. We were never allowed to take chances when the studio had us under contract. We were protected on and off the set. I was curious if Huston would try to stop me. Hell, no. He was delighted."[12]

Huston had a history of taking a lot out of his actors in his quest for realism. Barbara Walters said she thought he had a "mean streak."[13] In *Moby Dick* he'd endangered Gregory Peck.[14] Leo Genn and Richard Basehart were also put in the way of danger in that film.[15]

Roslyn gets her big scene after the horses are captured. The words she screams are heartfelt: "You liars! You're only living when you can watch something die! Kill everything, that's all you want! Why don't you just kill yourselves and be happy? I pity you."

Her acting is exceptionally good here. Huston shoots her from a distance. The scene is more effective that way. Even though she looks minute, her words roar across the desert. Huston was renowned for his close-ups but here the distance was right. It makes her seem like a voice lost in the wilderness. Miller didn't agree at first. He thought she wouldn't be seen or heard. Huston agreed to shoot the scene twice from different angles. When Miller watched them he had to agree Huston's way worked best.[16]

Ironically, for the early scenes in the film it was Miller who was campaigning for long shots. He wanted to convey isolation. Here the roles were reversed. Pyramid Lake had the look of people "living on the moon."[17] It was entirely appropriate.

Monroe always cared deeply about animals. When she lived in Connecticut with Miller there was a working farm on the land. One time a cow gave birth to a male calf. It wasn't wanted by the farmer so he arranged to have it killed for veal. She went hysterical when she heard this. On the same day she discovered a hawk trying to get at some swallow chicks nesting above her front porch. She threw rocks at it in an attempt to chase it away.[18] Miller said, "A wounded seagull could reduce her to weeping."[19] In 1958 she objected to a bull calf being led to an abattoir.[20] In New York one time she bought a set of caged pigeons from a group of teenagers and released them into the wild.[21] This was all fine but in *The Misfits* Roslyn has a dog that eats horsemeat. There's an inconsistency there.

This part of the film had its origins in the short story Miller wrote the previous year called "Please Don't Kill Anything." It features a man and woman watching fishermen hauling a net of fish into the

shore. The man is casual about it but the woman is nervous. When they're thrown onto the sand she becomes hysterical. He manages to throw some of the fish discarded by the fishermen back into the sea and they continue their stroll.

At the end of the story she looks up at him "like a little girl" even as she's smiling at him "in the way of a grown woman." Miller seems to be referencing the infantilism he sometimes saw in Monroe here. The closing lines are ironic. "Oh how I love you," the woman says to the man.[22] On the surface the issue has been resolved but, as was the case with Miller and Monroe, one can see problems down the line because of her concern for the natural world. It appears excessive. Her mental state also seems to be very fragile.

The happiness we're proffered is the kind one sometimes sees in the stories of Ernest Hemingway – a version that hints at its opposite. We feel the hero has more in common with the fishermen than he pretends, that he's been goaded into action by his lover rather than feeling the need for it himself. Earlier in the story we read: "He had to open the window at home once to let out a moth which ordinarily he would have swatted."[23] "Man has to eat and something's got to die, puss," he says to her. It sounds like the Gable line from the rodeo scene, with the added condescension of the "puss."[24] When a dog takes one of the fish from the water he says sarcastically, "The fish wishes you'd let it die in peace," making a mockery of her bleeding heart. All of these extracts take the power away from the "great happiness" the man is said to feel at the end of the story, making it seem like Miller is making fun of him too, as if he's her patsy.[25]

Monroe didn't appreciate the fact that Miller had her being so angry in the scene. If she'd been typecast as a dumb blonde in previous roles, here she thought she came across as a *crazy* dumb one.[26] She had a point. It was as if she wasn't capable of making her case without throwing a "screaming, crazy fit."[27]

"To think Arthur did this to me," she said. "He could have written me anything and he comes up with this. If that's what he thinks of me, then I'm not for him and he's not for me."[28]

From another point of view she seems to be more agitated than crazy. The nuances don't matter. It's the first time she's gone out of control and it's the climax of the film. We needed a big scene to showcase that.

Monroe might have given out about the scene but the sentiments Roslyn expressed in it were how she herself felt in real life. It was antithetical to the way Huston saw life. Huston was a friend of Ernest Hemingway. Monroe didn't like Hemingway. She saw only one type of character in his books, the macho man. "Those big tough guys are so sick," she said, "they're afraid of kindness and gentleness and beauty. They always want to kill something to prove themselves."[29] It's almost as if she's quoting Roslyn here. Of course there's much more to Hemingway's heroes than this. And indeed to Miller's ones.

Barbara Leaming believed the scene failed because it focused on the abstract idea of Roslyn objecting to an animal being killed. Miller would have been better off, she thought, to have Gay and Guido struggle with one another to gain her love. This is a good point. It would have given the film an "eternal triangle" theme rather than a "Please Don't Kill Anything" one.[30]

The scene took a lot out of Monroe. Huston asked for repeated takes. Was he seeking revenge on her for her unpunctuality? Strasberg whispered encouragement to her after each take. Someone else gave her "large spoonfuls of some vitamin-laden liquid."[31] One onlooker described her as sitting "grimly waiting, like a boxer in his corner trying to warm up so he'll be ready to fight at his best when the bell sounds. At the end she looked pale and exhausted; her entourage all but carried her away."[32]

Gable had a line to speak after Monroe finished screaming. As he went to say it, Clift lit a cigarette. Gable thought he was trying to upstage him. He became furious, storming off to his dressing room after the take. Taylor followed him inside. He said, "That goddamn fag stole the scene from me." But when he saw the rushes sometime later he changed his mind. He now saw Clift's action as perfect for the scene. Instead of debunking him he said he was "one hell of an actor."[33]

It's Perce who finally sets the horses free. Gay is furious with him. He recaptures their leader. This is the scene where he's dragged by the truck. It seems to fulfill his machismo. After capturing it he lets it go. He wants it to be his idea. Roslyn's outburst has had more of an effect on him than he said. Having performed the gracious act he's now free to reclaim her.

When Gay releases the horse he's going against the habits of a lifetime. He sacrifices his virility for the needs of the first truly

*Gable goes through his lines with a crew member. He came from the era where exactness was important, unlike his Method colleagues who preferred to improvise.*

gentle woman to have entered his life. By freeing the horse, in a sense, he's freeing himself.

Miller continued to revamp the script as the film entered its final stages. He was writing "on the hoof," as he'd been doing all along, putting snatches of dialogue in as they allied with his life or as things with Monroe changed. This wasn't what Gable was used to. He'd spent his life learning prepared lines that didn't change. He was amenable to variation but only if it went so far.

He reached his breaking point now. "No more changes," he said to Huston. Huston told him Miller had written a great end scene to the film. He asked him to consider it. It would be the last set of new dialogue he'd have to learn. When Gable read the scene he liked it so much he agreed to do it.

The original ending had Gay being unable to trap the horse. He doesn't let it go willingly. It beats him. Afterwards he lies prostrate on the lake bed. Perce and Roslyn bring him back to the town. Roslyn says that if he dies, she will too. This wouldn't do for he-man Gable. He asked Miller to rewrite it. The eventual ending is much fluffier.

Monroe is dressed in virgin white in the last scene. It contrasts sharply with the funeral black of her opening one with Kevin McCarthy. The symbolism is perhaps too obvious. She's more natural in cowgirl jeans (she'd already worn these in *Clash by Night*) and the dress she wears with the red cherries and the little bows on top.

"How do you find your way back in the dark?" she asks Gay. "Just head for that big star straight on," he replies. "The highway's under it. It'll take us right home." It's a great line, maybe Gable's best since "Frankly, my dear, I don't give a damn." It's also a perfect ending for the film. Roslyn has said "you" instead of "we" but he uses the plural with "us." The big star is Venus, the goddess of love. She's come back to him. Together they'll find "another way to be alive." One that's better than wages.

The scene was ironic in view of what was happening off-screen: "Gable, Miller's surrogate, wins Marilyn at the very moment Miller loses her."[34]

Miller wasn't sure if Gable had been expressive enough in the scene. He asked him what his own view was. He was supposed to look at Monroe with "a mounting look of love in his eyes." Gable said, "You can't overdo it. It's being magnified hundreds of times on the screen." When Miller looked at the rushes he realized he was right. The affection that was "undetectable a few feet away" was easily visible to him now.[35]

Monroe wanted them to break up at the end. Miller thought that would be too downbeat.[36] He didn't want to carry a negative frame of mind about his relationship with Monroe into the film. Until now he'd only emphasized the positives. A sad ending would also have hurt its box office potential. There was already enough grimness in it.

Clift thought Miller wanted the film to end happily in some kind of fantasy projection that he and Monroe would too. From that point of view it was wish fulfillment on his part: "But their marriage is over and he might as well face it." The pairing with Gable was wrong for Clift: "It's like a girl going with her father. Arthur's got it wrong."[37] Clift thought Perce would have been a better fit for her: "My character represented something new – the future."[38]

*The happy threesome – but a world of pain resided behind those smiles.*

Miller hoped that by living through the role, Monroe might arrive "at some threshold of faith and confidence."[39] He hoped art would turn into life, that she would become Roslyn by proxy through the film. This was a wild hope. It was far too late for such a miracle. Monroe could never head for any "big star" with him.

Miller had another reason for wanting things to end happily: "*The Misfits* is the first work of mine where the hero doesn't die." He added, "I'm feeling my way towards a way to live."[40] This is like something Gay would have said in the film. Maybe Miller was morphing into him just as Monroe had morphed into Roslyn.

Both Gay and Roslyn were approaching the future with a tentative attitude as far as he was concerned. Roslyn "wants to rely on people while at the same time being very suspicious of them." Gay believed most people disappointed you "but there's always someone who won't."[41]

One could delve into their various perspectives forever and still arrive at no conclusions. In the final analysis does it really matter if Roslyn ends up with Gay or Perce? "In a Huston movie," Alice

*A jubilant Gay and Roslyn embrace as they plan to head for the "big star"
over the highway after all the months of stress.*

McIntyre once wrote, "it's always the camera that gets the girl. He
delivers his leading lady to the audience rather than to the leading
man."[42] So neither Gay nor Perce gets her.

She belongs to all of us.

# Wrapping Up

The sky became overcast. The lake changed to the silver-gray color of fall in the desert.

The birth of Gable's child grew closer. Kay drove out to the set on September 29 with an antique child's cradle she'd bought. She wanted to show her him. Gable said to Eve Arnold, "I see Kathleen got her cradle." Arnold didn't know what he was talking about. It was the first time he'd mentioned her pregnancy to anyone. "We didn't want to make it public," he said to her, "She lost one before."[1]

He was very excited about his forthcoming child. One day he asked Huston to be excused from the set when Kay was seeing the baby doctor but Huston refused. He said he needed him for a scene. In the end he wasn't needed at all. Gable went into a rage about that. It was one of the few times Huston saw him "blowing up."[2]

The weekend before location filming ended, Monroe went to see Ella Fitzgerald in concert in San Francisco. Accompanying her were Strasberg, Roberts, May Reis and Paula Flanagan. DiMaggio wasn't in town but she spent some time with his brother and sister. She was close to both of them. The short trip confirmed her in her decision to divorce Miller.

There was a joint birthday party for Clift and Miller on October 17. It was Miller's 45th and Clift's 40th. Monroe refused to sing "Happy Birthday" to Miller at it.[3] She went to a casino afterwards to shoot craps with Huston. She said to him, "What do you ask the dice for?" He said, "Don't think. Just throw. It's the story of your life."[4] Huston thought she had a lucky roll but didn't know what to do with it.[5] Maybe that was the story of her life too.

Location shooting finished the following day. Miller and Monroe went back to the Mapes in separate cars. He thought she looked calm as she left the desert with Strasberg. Suddenly all the trauma seemed to be gone. Had he dramatized it too much? He thought she was resilient. She could be "like a milk-fed high school girl hours after peering over the edge into death's very jaws." Underneath that frailty there was a wall of steel. "I'm more than one person," she said, "and I act differently each time."[6] Such schizophrenia – real or imagined – helped her acting but caused havoc with her personality.

By the end of October everyone was back in Hollywood for scenes requiring back projection and special effects. There would be no more blips, no more temper tantrums, no more forest fires or electrical failures. The elements were quelled in Paramount Studios as well. The director was back in charge. He could be an auteur now.

For Miller the experience of ending the film was strange because of the manner in which his relationship with Monroe had collapsed during the course of it: "I made a present of it to her and I left it without her."[7]

After he got back to Hollywood he wondered why things had ended as they did or if they could have ended any other way. He drove down Sunset Boulevard remembering a dinner he'd had there once with her. She'd gone in disguise to avoid being pestered by crowds but the plan backfired. They were refused a table, being regarded as nobodies. Now he was a nobody again, driving a "clunky rented green American Motors mess."[8]

The world returned to itself. It was time to forget about his mustangers and get back to real life. The Nixon-Kennedy debates were taking place. Maybe a new dawn would begin for America if Kennedy was elected President. He wanted to get his mind onto such issues.

That was easier said than done. There were almost as many articles in the papers about his strained relationship with Monroe as there were about the future of the country.

Clift was in a more relaxed frame of mind as he left the set. "Two weeks ago I was forty," he told Joe Hyams, "but I feel my life is just beginning." He was one of the few people who'd enjoyed making the film. He was pleased with his performance and hadn't been frustrated by Monroe. He hadn't had to wait as long for her as Gable. She always seemed to trip along to his scenes. Maybe that

Un canto a la vida......
una explosión
de amor......

Seven Arts Productions presenta a

CLARK · MARILYN · MONTGOMERY

# Gable ⋆ Monroe · Clift

en la producción de John Huston

# Los Inadaptados

(THE MISFITS)

Con

Thelma Ritter · Eli Wallach · Argumento de Arthur Miller · Producción de Frank E. Taylor · Dirección de John Huston

Música de Alex North

UNITED ARTISTS — Distribuida por ARTISTAS UNIDOS

was because she didn't have to work at them as much. They'd had that almost clairvoyant understanding of one another.

Gable made a vow to slow down from now on. "I'm taking time off until the baby is born. No more pictures now." He wanted to be at home for the birth, "and to be there for a good many months afterwards."[9]

He said to Huston, "All I want out of life is what Langland wants – to see that kid of mine born." He was chuffed that he was about to be a father at his age: "I guess there's life in the old boy yet."[10]

Because Huston edited the film as it was shot, he was able to show it to Gable in its entirety. He loved it. In his view it was the best work he'd done since *Gone With the Wind*.[11] It didn't bother him that it came in half a million over budget and forty days behind schedule. "If the studio is unhappy," he told Huston, "I'll buy it for $4 million."[12] It was the most expensive black and white film to be made since *Ben-Hur* in 1925. Monroe was estimated to have cost it over $200,000 because of all the delays.[13]

Miller's reaction to the it was less ecstatic than Gable's. He said it had no plot: "All the characters do is react to one another." A voice boomed from the back of the projection room, "That's its strength, Arthur."[14]

Despite all the problems he'd had with it, Huston was sad that it was over. "Each picture is a little lifetime," he said, "and then one day it's over, never to be gone back into."[15]

The wrap party was held on November 14. It was subdued. Nobody was quite sure what they'd done. Was it a love story? An adventure? A psychological drama? The shoot was so tense it made it difficult to look outside it. Monroe wasn't as sure of her performance as were Gable and Clift. It owed too much to a man who'd put the wrong kinds of things into it.

Gable didn't attend the party as he was feeling unwell. The following day he got a pain in his chest while he was changing a tire on his jeep. He left the jeep on the road and went inside to rest. He'd been getting pains like this for a few days. He hadn't mentioned them to Kay. He thought she had enough on her mind thinking about the baby. He imagined it was just indigestion.

He'd been busy since coming home. Earlier that day he'd been wrestling with his stepchildren.[16] He felt great then. He'd also been speeding down the motorway in his Mercedes at 148 miles an hour.[17]

An ambulance was called. He was taken to hospital. Coronary thrombosis was diagnosed. He had a clot in one of the arteries leading to his heart. Six nurses attended him.[18] He was put on a heart monitor.

He was jolly in the hospital but Kay was worried enough to insist on staying with him. She slept in a truckle bed in his room. The world waited for news of his condition. President Eisenhower was said to have sent him a telegram saying, "Be a good boy, Clark, and do what the doctors tell you." That wasn't true. They weren't on first name terms. But Eisenhower did write him a letter from the White House expressing his concern.[19]

He was glad to have Kay near him. The pregnancy was going well and she was taking good care of herself. One day when a doctor was examining him he asked him for his stethoscope. He put it to her stomach to see if he could hear the baby's heartbeat.

A week later his specialist had him taken off his heart monitor. It was felt he was over the worst. He'd even begun having his meals catered from Chasen's. But on the evening of November 16 he took a turn. Kay had just left his room. She wasn't on the truckle bed anymore. He was flipping through the pages of a magazine when his head fell back against the pillows of the bed. The nurse who was attending him saw him yawn. Then his head dropped.[20]

He was dead. Just like that. The King of Hollywood had slipped into oblivion while reading a magazine.

Kay didn't believe it when she got the news. She became hysterical. Charging back into the room, she held him in her arms for a reported two hours.[21]

The world was shocked. Nobody had an inkling he'd had heart trouble. Only Eve Arnold knew he'd had a previous coronary.[22]

Joan Crawford said he should have been taken to hospital long before he was. A friend of hers had seen the abandoned jeep outside his house. He'd been driving by and became alerted by it. He stopped his car and knocked on his door. When he was invited inside he saw Gable was panting. He didn't think Kay understood the gravity of the situation.[23]

Monroe was woken with the news at 4 a.m. She was traumatized. There were rumors her difficulty on the set had caused Gable so much stress it brought on the attack. Such rumors traumatized her more. "Why didn't he tell me?" she said. "Why didn't he say something?" I'd have done anything for him. Anything. All he had to do was ask me to be on time. That's all. He always said, 'That's all right, honey' – like he understood."[24]

Monroe suffered abuse in the following weeks. People sometimes stopped their cars as she walked down the street. They rolled down their windows and shouted out, "How does it feel to be a murderer?" She took their words on board, saying, "I know it's my fault he's dead."[25] She guilt-tripped herself about casting him in the mold of her father, a man who walked out on her and had to be punished almost Oedipally in the guise of Gable.[26] There were suggestions she'd attempted suicide in her grief.[27]

The allegations didn't stop there. Once the gossip mill ground into motion it was like a runaway train. She was said to have tried to seduce Gable on the set of the film, her efforts being interrupted by Kay.[28] There's no evidence to support this and it doesn't ring true to everything else we know about their relationship during the shoot.

She remembered the way his moustache tickled her when he kissed her, how he was so gracious to her, always getting a chair for her to sit on when such a gesture would have been the last thing on anyone else's mind.

Some people blamed Huston for his death. They said his exertion during the roping scenes in the film were what brought on his coronary. Hedda Hopper rang Robert Mitchum and told him Huston killed Gable. Mitchum replied that he'd tried to kill him too. Huston defended himself by saying a stunt double was used for the more strenuous scenes. Miller rowed in behind him, saying that Gable brought it on himself with all his smoking. He was a three pack a day man.[29]

Monroe wouldn't be consoled. "I kept him waiting!" she kept saying, like a mantra. And then, "We were planning another movie together."[30]

Kay put the blame more on Monroe than Huston. She thought the hours of boredom he spent waiting for her spurred him on to

*Monroe always blamed herself for Gable's death but John Huston was more culpable for the strenuous action sequences he had him do.*

do more stunts in the roping scenes than he might otherwise have done.[31]

A few days before filming ended, Gable was alleged to have said, "What the hell is that girl's problem? God damn it I like her but she's so damned unprofessional. I damn near went nuts up there in Reno waiting for her to show. Christ, she didn't show up until after lunch some days. I'm glad this picture's finished.... She damn near gave me a heart attack."[32] This alleged quotation is from James Spada's biography of Peter Lawford. It sounds fabricated. In an interview he did just days before he died Gable said she might have arrived late at the studio sometimes but when Marilyn was there she was really there. "Other actresses can arrive early and never be there."[33]

Everyone seemed to have a different view. They changed by the day. Another theory was that the attack was brought on by grief over the death of Gable's friend Ward Bond. Bond had died on November 5.

All the legends were dying. Bogart went in 1957, Tyrone Power the following year and Errol Flynn in 1959. Now Gable. Who was left? *The New York Times* wrote that he was "as certain as that sunrise."[34] Where was the sunrise now?

Huston was even more generous in his eulogy: "He was one of the few holdovers from the days of the champs. His career had the same sweep and color as Dempsey's ring career. You can put Gable's name on a list with the Babes, the Galloping Ghosts, the Flying Finns. They called him King out here and he rated the title. His throne, I fear, will remain empty for some time."[35]

Monroe didn't go to the funeral. This wasn't only from guilt. She didn't want the attention to be on her rather than Gable. He lay in a closed casket. He'd told Kay, "I don't want a lot of strangers looking down at my wrinkles and my big fat belly."[36]

He was buried beside Carole Lombard, the greatest love of his life. He believed he'd see her soon, that she'd be waiting for him in the great beyond. The two of them lay side by side in a crypt in the Sanctuary of Trust in Forest Lawn Cemetery in Glendale, California, twinned for eternity.

*A love match made in heaven – but Gable was in his grave before the film was released.*

# Parting of the Ways

"We were no longer man and wife," Miller said of himself and Monroe after *The Misfits* was put in the can. "The film was there but the marriage was not."[1]

He'd written the story on which it was based when he was ending his first marriage. The screenplay ended his second one. He wrote it to save the marriage to Monroe. Instead it destroyed it.

Who was to blame? Both of them and neither. Monroe expected too much from him. She wanted him to be her father, her lover, her friend, her agent, "and above all, somebody who would never criticize her for anything…I don't know if that human being exists."[2] Monroe said, "I put Arthur through a lot but he put me through a lot too."[3] Maybe it was as simple as that.

She knew she was no angel and confessed as much: "A lot of people like to think of me as innocent so that's the way I behave to them but if they saw the real me they'd hate me."[4]

Miller told his parents his marriage was over on November 7. They were shocked. He'd kept his problems with Monroe secret from them over the years. Later that month he resigned as director of Marilyn Monroe Productions. May Reis left soon after him. She'd been very close to him and found it difficult to work for Monroe without him. Rupert Allan was replaced by Pat Newcombe as Monroe's personal press representative. Monroe had argued with Newcombe during the filming of *Bus Stop* but they reconciled now. Allan went off to Monaco to work for Princess Grace.

They announced their divorce on Armistice Day, November 11. It was major news. Monroe was besieged by reporters. One of them shoved his microphone into her mouth in his over-enthusiastic search for a quote. She suffered a chipped tooth as a result.[5] Five days later, *France-Dimanche* carried the headline, "Montand the Reason for Marilyn's Divorce."[6] The Soviet magazine *Nedelya* put it differently: "She found in Arthur Miller what she lacked.

He wrote scripts for her and made her a real actress. Marilyn paid him back by leaving him."[7]

There seemed to be as many variations on the split as there were publications. *The Daily News* had the headline, "Miller Walks Out On Marilyn."[8] He checked in to the Chelsea Hotel while she went back to their 57th Street apartment.

*The New York Times* was less sensationalistic. The reason they divorced, it said, was because they were polar opposites: "She's not just a star, she's an institution. She must constantly be in the center of excitement and activity." Miller's work, on the other hand, "requires him to be completely alone and away from the stresses of showbusiness."[9]

When Monroe went into the apartment she got a surprise. All Miller had left behind him was a portrait of her – his favorite one.[10] It was a strange thing to leave. Was he trying to blot her out of his mind? Expunge even the best parts of her?

Miller got the Roxbury home. Before he went back there he spent some time living pseudonomously at the Chelsea Hotel. Monroe rang him one night. She asked him if she could go there to collect some of her things. She wanted to see him one last time but he wasn't interested. He told her she was welcome to call anytime but there was no guarantee he'd be there. Why would she need him to be? She knew where the key was.

She rang another night. She said, "Are you coming home?" as if they were still a couple. He couldn't understand it after all she'd put him through. It was as if nothing happened. She was needy for him. The past was wiped out "like a color photo of violence that had been left too long in the sun." He couldn't share her amnesia. Returning to the old life would have been "like trying to die backwards."[11]

He'd stayed with her until she began to threaten his hold on sanity. She was like a drowning woman who was trying to bring him down with her. The intensity with which she'd loved him at the beginning had now turned inside out. He was her enemy but she was acting as if they could be an item again.

They should have separated long before they did. The film kept them together but in the process increased the tension. Both of

them knew the marriage was over before the movie began shooting. Keeping up the façade for the crew, most of whom knew what was going on anyway, was a farce. Their body language and their silences, not to mention the heated words heard by Wallach through the walls of the Mapes, made it clear even to those on the fringes that they were headed for the divorce courts.

"Was all that torture worth the result?" Miller asked.[12] Monroe had a different take on it: "When Arthur saw me first I was an innocent among the Hollywood wolves. I became his student in life and literature. When the monster showed, he couldn't believe it. I put him through a lot and vice versa. Marriage would have been easier with a partygoer."[13] Indeed, but would a partygoer have been faithful to her? Would he not have been like Montand?

Susan Strasberg thought most of the problems in the marriage were Miller's fault. She believed he saw her as a sex symbol and couldn't deal with her sensitive side. She thought he was jealous of her relationship to the Strasbergs because they were like surrogate parents to her. As for Monroe's feelings for Miller, she'd "fallen in love with a part of herself she didn't know. Each of them had married their opposite. Sometimes that worked but if you were too opposite it didn't.[14]

Strasberg had mixed feelings about Monroe's performance in *The Misfits*. She thought it would have worked better if Miller and Huston had been more empathetic to her during the shoot.

"What Arthur and Huston didn't comprehend," she said, "was that Marilyn was like an Aeolian harp, a fine-tuned instrument so sensitive that the ancient Greeks cold place them on hilltops and play music at the slightest breeze through them. With her super-sensitivity she could pick up thoughts, whispers, lies."[15]

Monroe resumed classes at the Actors Studio in December. At this time she was also receiving daily counseling from Marianne Kris. Kris was a childhood friend of Sigmund Freud's daughter Anna.

Eve Arnold called to her apartment one day with some photographs she'd taken on the set. Monroe had to approve or disapprove them. Every time she saw one with Miller she put an X through it. One day while Arnold was with her another woman called to interview her. Monroe was wearing a see-through robe at the time with nothing underneath. She asked the woman if it was okay to brush her hair. The woman said that was fine, whereupon Monroe started brushing her *pubic* hair.[16] Was this the woman who wanted to leave Lorelei behind to play Grushenka?

Another day she gave a photo of herself to Rob Slatzer, inscribing it, "From one misfit to another."[17] In mid-December she did an interview with *Cosmopolitan* magazine in which she said she was "delighted" to have Miller close by.[18] She was playing a double game on the charade that they were friends for the sake of the film, a game with herself and with him. Did she want him back? Did she still hate him? Nobody knew, least of all herself.

He distanced himself from her more after the divorce. Nothing else was an option. The psychological cost would have been too high. "If I hadn't done this," he said, "I would have been dead."[19]

Coming up to Christmas Monroe heard that Yves Montand was going to be in New York on a flight stopover. She tried to meet him but he wasn't interested.[20] She was reaching for anything now, any shard from her past, but he'd moved on. He'd completed *Sanctuary* and, like Miller, seemed more focused on his career than his personal life.

She tried to contact him by phone, telegram and mail. She sent him a dog-eared postcard that said, "I love you." He didn't reply, busy as he was with his work and anxious to move on from their dalliance. When he finished *Sanctuary* he embarked on Anatole Litvak's *Goodbye Again* with Ingrid Bergman and Anthony Perkins. After that he signed up for *My Geisha* with Shirley MacLaine. He'd now made four Hollywood films in a row, thereby establishing himself as a fixture in the industry outside France. This had always been his ambition.

Miller now started seeing Inge Morath. It wasn't premeditated. When he ran into her on a street one day in New York he couldn't even remember her name. His head was so scrambled with the

Monroe problems he was only vaguely aware of her clicking her camera. But now he got interested. After she went off he asked Nan Taylor for her phone number and he rang her to ask her out. She said she'd meet him for dinner and things took off from there.

Neither of them wanted to get into a relationship too quickly so their dates were subdued. She was slow to commit to him because he seemed so serious. She was serious too, also having a failed marriage behind her. Both of them felt like damaged goods. That made them weirdly compatible. Miller told her he was "preoccupied by endings."[21] But a month after he announced his divorce from Monroe he moved in with her. In time she saw he wasn't as serious as he made out.

Monroe wasn't pleased at the idea of Morath being in Miller's life. After originally suspecting Angela Allen to be his mistress, she now realized she was totally wrong about that. Men had always pulled the wool over her eyes. She didn't appreciate the speed with which the relationship with Morath progressed. Had his marriage meant so little to him that he was able to move on to another woman so quickly? Morath made her feel like "a negated sex symbol."[22]

Christmas approached. Monroe gave Pat Newcombe a fur coat as a gift. It was extravagant as she was such a recent employee.

She also gave gifts to the children of Miller and DiMaggio. She didn't just want to be a stepmother to Miller's daughter and DiMaggio's son but rather a friend. "They're from broken homes too," she pointed out.[23]

DiMaggio sent her a bouquet of poinsettias. When she asked him why, he said, "Who the hell else do you have in the world [but me]?" He was comfortable enough with her to be able to make jokes like that. They spent a lot of the Christmas season together. At times it seemed as if they hadn't split up at all. She didn't blame him for divorcing her in 1954. "I'd have divorced me too," she said.[24]

Billy Wilder said her marriage to DiMaggio failed when he realized he married Marilyn Monroe and that her marriage to Miller failed when he realized he didn't.[25] It's an interesting point. One man wanted the woman, the other the icon.

He became an anchor that she tethered herself to. The things that had once bothered her about him, like his stay-at-home personality, suddenly became desirable to her. Anything had to be better than Miller's coldness.

She gave an interview in which she appeared to be surprisingly calm about the divorce. "Mr. Miller is a wonderful man," she told reporters, "and a great writer. It just didn't work out that we should be husband and wife. But everybody I ever loved I still love a little."[26]

Susan Strasberg thought Monroe missed Miller more than she realized: "For almost five years he'd been the maypole around which she had danced and played. When he'd lost his center, bent too much in the prevailing wind, Marilyn had begun to panic and lash out."[27]

That lashing was now replaced with loneliness. It seemed to be her destiny no matter how many men lusted after her. She was an icon plowing a lone furrow. "I belonged to the audience," she said, "not because of my talent or even because I was beautiful but because I never belonged to any one individual."[28]

Her depression deepened. When her friend Norman Rosten phoned her she didn't pick up. Her voice was frequently slurred when he did. The only people she allowed to visit her were the Strasbergs. She talked a lot about suicide. When Pat Newcomb took her for a ride on the Staten Island Ferry one day, she stared at the water as if she was thinking of jumping into it.[29]

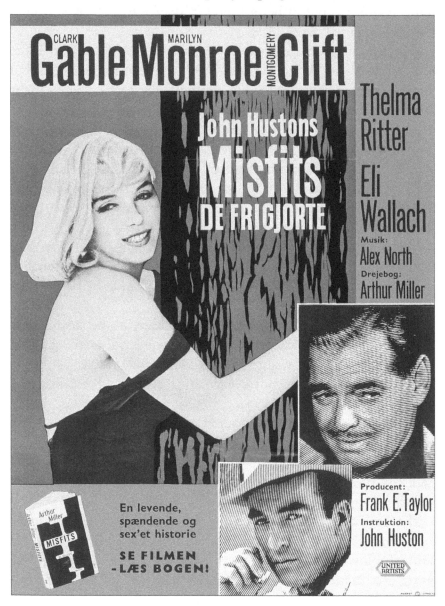

# Reception and Fallout

The premiere was held on January 11, 1961. Monroe didn't attend. When the lights came up, Miller said, "I made a present of this to her and I left it without her."[1] He had mixed feelings about the film. It made him both sad and happy: "What's very sad is that I wrote it to make Marilyn feel good, and for her it resulted in complete collapse. But at the same time I was glad it was done because her dream was to be a serious actress."[2]

A week later Monroe went to Mexico with Pat Newcomb and her attorney Aaron Frosch to secure her divorce from Miller. It was the day of John F. Kennedy's inauguration. She thought that would deflect attention from her but it didn't. She was all over the papers and even on the radio.[3] On the way back to New York she stopped in Dallas between flights to watch the inauguration. The location was ominous. Kennedy was assassinated there two years later.

The film was released on February 1, the day that would have been Gable's sixtieth birthday. It was an unsubtle ploy on United Artist's part to exploit a tragedy but it didn't work. A similar tactic was attempted by Warner Brothers after James Dean died. *Giant* received a Best Picture nomination on that occasion. *The Misfits* didn't on this one.

Monroe attended the premiere with Harry Belafonte. Miller didn't go. He went to dinner at Frank Taylor's house instead.

Reviews were mixed. *The New York Times* thought it was too sentimental, that the characters didn't develop and that the film itself had little direction, it didn't add up to a point.[4] It was dismissed by another reviewer as a film about three men trying to get Monroe into bed – and they were all Miller. It was "New Wavish" but lacked an even tempo.[5]

People were mostly confused by it. It was a different kind of western, a different kind of Monroe and a different kind of Reno. Where were the hookers? Where was the gambling? Norman

Mailer said it moved "like a wounded caterpillar." He described it as a film about "a dog-eat-horse society." He thought there was "no blueprint" to the line of Monroe's heart. Instead she seemed to shimmer on the screen.[6] Her effect in the film ended up being more that of a presence than a woman, "not an actor but an essence."[7]

Some reviewers praised her for capturing Roslyn's "quiet desperation."[8] Others felt Huston fixated on her breasts and rear end.[9] Still others thought she tried too hard and lost the thing that people loved – her spontaneity: "You see all the Strasberg lessons going through her head."[10] The combination of this with Miller's "heavy-handed allegorizing" proved too daunting for those who just wanted a straight story.[11]

Alice McIntye of *Esquire* thought she was "like nothing human you have ever seen or dreamed. She is astonishingly white, so radically pale that in her presence you can look at others about as easily as you explore the darkness around the moon. Indeed, there seems the awful possibility in the various phases of her person that MM is a manifestation of the White Goddess herself: disdaining all lingerie and dressed in tight, white silk emblazoned with countless red cherries, she becomes at once the symbol of impartial and eternal availability, who yet remains forever pure – and a potentially terrible goddess whose instinct could also deal death and whose smile, when she directs it clearly at you, is exquisitely, heartbreakingly sweet."[12]

The nastiest review she received was from the writer who described her as resembling "an aunt of Mae West's who has been eating temperately at Luchow's."[13] Another one said her childlike mannerisms distracted from the complexities of her character.[14]

The scene where she embraced the tree outside Guido's house caused ripples of dissent from the Catholic Church. Some priests believed she seemed to be getting sexual pleasure from pushing herself against it.[15] Huston thought this was ludicrous. He threatened to identify the priests who made the charge. They backed off as a result.[16]

Miller said there was no room in the script for a run-of-the-mill personality: "I don't remember a picture that depends quite so much on oddity. If anyone were average, it wouldn't work."[17] One could also argue that it doesn't work for precisely that reason. He's overplaying his hand if everyone is odd. Ubiquity makes it into a different kind of normal.

The critics reached a consensus on one point: The literary dialogue was no substitute for the flimsiness of the back stories that were given to the characters. At its worst this came across as the overzealous effort of a playwright trying to inject drama into a medium he was unfamiliar with.

Miller's misfits, one writer contended, "strive to discover the secret of self-realization in an uncongenial environment, distorting their banal diction into unrecognizable shapes. Their resolve to codify a vocabulary of integrity produces language that is neither natural nor rational."[18]

Put another way, Miller suffered from a tendency to constantly over-think his material. Roger Angell wrote, "When, at the end of the picture, Mr. Gable's rueful cowboy, the last of the Western giants, ropes and wrestles down the last free stallion and then cuts it loose, we realize with disappointment that we have been on the Plains of Allegory all along, that the drumming of hoofs does not obscure the clack of the author's typewriter."[19]

Huston was disappointed at the reaction. He put so much into it, it hurt all the more to think he'd missed the target. It was actually his favorite of all his films.[20] Was it now destined to die a death at the box office? Miller never thought of it as "first run" material. He expected it might do well in art house cinemas. Huston had more mainstream ambitions for it, even in black and white.[21]

Monroe was disappointed too. Despite complaints about Miller, she knew he'd given her a platform from which she could develop into a different kind of actress. But if her maiden voyage in that direction was deemed pretentious, where would it lead her?

Sitting around her apartment in a state of depression, she drank Bloody Marys. She worried about her face and figure and played records of Frank Sinatra. There were times she thought she'd like to have married him. Now they were just friends. Was this her lot, to end up being mere friends with former lovers? Or even former husbands like DiMaggio?

She was losing weight. She started to think there might be something wrong with her. Deciding to have herself checked out, she had Marianne Kris drive her to the Payne-Whitney clinic on February 5.

She signed herself in under the name Faye Miller, a not very subtle pseudonym. Maybe it didn't matter. She was one of the most recognizable people in the country. But she wasn't prepared for the prurient curiosity of the staff and patients. Maybe she should have expected this after a lifetime of being preyed on by the paparazzi.

She thought she was going to an ordinary hospital but it turned out to be a psychiatric one. It was nicknamed "The rich people's crazy house."[22] Her experience there was Kafkaesque. As soon as she was admitted, her handbag and personal effects were taken from her. She then spent 48 hours in a padded cell. The experience terrified her.

According to a member of staff she took off all her clothes at one stage and stood naked at a window.[23] Another time she threw a chair through a glass door. She did this to try and convince them she was mad: "I got the idea from a movie I made once called *Don't Bother to Knock*." Her attitude was, "If you're going to treat me like a nut I'll act like one."[24] The incident caused her to be threatened with a straitjacket. Such a prospect brought back a terror of insanity that she'd had all her life. Her grandmother was psychologically unhinged and so was her mother. She believed she had a streak of insanity too. She wrote a letter to the Strasbergs about the "idiot doctors" who were treating her and the "nutty people" she saw everywhere.[25] She begged them to rescue her. She also phoned Joe DiMaggio.

He rallied to her call, arriving at the hospital one day and demanding that his "wife" be released. He said he'd tear the place asunder if she wasn't.

Her plight became public news. She was extremely disturbed by the newspapers.[26] On February 10 she was transferred to the Columbia Presbyterian Medical Center. It was the kind of hospital she'd thought she'd be in from the outset when Kris dropped her off. She didn't blame Kris. She'd been misinformed too.

She spent three weeks resting there. During the course of her stay she received a telegram from Marlon Brando which lifted her spirits. It was simple but profound: "Dear Marilyn, The best reappraisals are made in the worst crisis. It has happened to all of us in relative degrees. Be glad of it and don't be afraid of being afraid. It can only help. Relax and enjoy it. I send you my thoughts and my warmest affections, Marlon."[27] She'd had an affair with him in the past. He always held her in high esteem.

In the following week she became more and more dependent on medication. At one stage Greenson got his daughter to deliver Nembutal to her home. This was a breach of patient confidentiality. By now he'd become star-struck by her. He wanted a relationship with her that was beyond medicine. She became like a daughter to him. "Her prime need," Greenson said, "was the warmth and affection our family could give her. She'd never experienced it as a child and her fame made it impossible when she was older."[28] Hymen Engelberg said their relationship was far too intimate for impartial judgment to be administered.[29]

Greenson saw her for consultations every other day. Some of them lasted up to five hours. Many were held in his home. She ate with his family and sometimes stayed overnight. She'd always had a wish to belong to a "real" family because of her orphaned past and he tapped into that need. The fact that she'd confided all her insecurities to him gave him an added weapon over her. If Miller used these insecurities to create the screenplay of *The Misfits*, Greenson used them to enhance his bank balance and his celebrity status. He even persuaded her to use his brother-in-law, Mickey Rudin, as her lawyer.

They talked about the film sometimes. She even wrote letters to him about it. In one of them she said, "Men are climbing to the moon but they don't seem to understand the beating of the human heart." She thought this was its real theme, that it got lost in all the script changes and directorial distortions.[30]

Gable's son was born in March. Kay had miscarried her last baby despite taking every precaution. She didn't take as many precautions this time but she had no problems with the delivery. The christening wasn't held until June. She invited Monroe to it. It was only 124 days since Gable died. Emotions were still raw but the pair had become friends in the interim. Kay forgave Monroe's behavior on the set of the film and any impact it might have had on his death. "Clark never said an unkind word about you," she told Monroe.[31] Two months earlier she'd sent her a letter which read, "I miss Clark each day more. I'll never get over this great loss. But God has blessed me with three great children and precious memories." The other two children were from her previous marriage. This one, whom she called John Clark, was the only child she had by Gable. After he was born she sent Monroe a copy of the first photograph she took of him.

Monroe held the baby for so long at the christening party she made the other guests uncomfortable. She was dressed in black. Was her mind on Gable rather than the baby? Was this the dress she'd intended wearing to his funeral if she went to it?

The christening returned Monroe to thoughts of her failure to conceive a child herself. She'd become pregnant three times while married to Miller but miscarried each time. She came to regard this as punishment for her past, for the abortions she'd had in the forties when her career was all she could think of and motherhood the last thing on her mind.

Where would she transfer her attentions now? To her career? To a man who'd love her despite her inability to have a child? Montand and Miller were gone. DiMaggio, despite his kindness, was always going to be more friend than lover.

She started seeing Frank Sinatra again in the summer but he didn't show any interest in marrying her. She became like a mascot of Sinatra's Rat Pack, an honorary member he could drink and have fun with without thinking of any lasting commitment. He enjoyed her company like other Rat Pack members – Dean Martin, Peter Lawford, Sammy Davis Jr. – but he didn't consider her marriage material. Lawford was married to Pat Kennedy, Jack's sister. Sinatra referred to him as "Brother-in-Lawford."

Monroe didn't make any films in 1961. Her health came against her. She had bleeding from her uterus and an ulcerated colon. In May she underwent a gynecological operation in Los Angeles. Doctors discovered her Fallopian tubes were blocked following poor surgery after an abortion in the past. She claimed to have had fourteen abortions in all.[32]

Sinatra did a concert at the Sands in Las Vegas in mid-June. She was sleeping with him at the time. Eddie Fisher attended too. He said more people were watching Monroe than Sinatra: "She swayed back and forth to the music and pounded her hands on the stage, her breasts falling out of her low-cut dress. She was so beautiful – and so drunk. She came to a party later that evening. Sinatra made no secret of his displeasure at her behavior."[33]

Sinatra had strung women along before Monroe, most notably Lauren Bacall, breaking off an engagement to her for no better reason than she leaked it to the press. For someone who could invest songs with such emotion he often lacked empathy in his private life. Reports suggest he had a short fuse when it came to Monroe, especially when she spoke of how lost she felt during her childhood. His response to this, more often than not, was an exasperated, "Not that again!"[34]

At the end of June she had her gall bladder removed. She left New York for Hollywood in August. In October she started an affair with Robert Kennedy after meeting him at Peter Lawford's beach house. She attended a dinner there the following month at which John F. Kennedy was present. Like Robert, he was Lawford's brother-in-law. They slept together. She told Ralph Roberts, "I made his back feel a lot better."[35] Kennedy suffered from chronic back pain all his life. She also was alleged to have had an affair with Robert Kennedy.

She was drawn to the Kennedys like a moth to a flame but there was never going to be anything lasting for her in either relationship. Even if they weren't married, the combination of actress and politician didn't look good on paper. Her affiliation with Sinatra made such a combination toxic in Robert's case. As Attorney General he was getting tough on organized crime. Sinatra's Mob connections made him anathema to him.

Robert, the story went, had been sent to Monroe by Jack to terminate his relationship with her. Instead of that, he was smitten by her charms and began his own affair with her. The situation was untenable. Monroe said she felt like a piece of meat being tossed between them.[36] Her relationship with Jack was rumored to have threatened his marriage to Jackie. Jackie was even said to have changed her voice to make Jack attractive to her, mimicking Monroe's "breathy whispering."[37]

# Goodbye Norma Jean

The next year began badly for Monroe. On the first day of 1962 she learned of the death of her lawyer friend Jerry Giesler. He'd handled her divorce from DiMaggio. She then heard that Inge Morath was pregnant and that Miller planned to marry her. The news had a devastating effect on her. She sank into a gloom.

The author Fred Guiles asked Miller if he thought Monroe's depression resulted from her knowledge of Morath's pregnancy. He replied defensively that it hadn't because she always knew it was she who'd had the problem when it came to reproducing rather than him.[1] That wasn't the point. What Guiles was getting at was the fact that Monroe would have seen the quickness of Miller and Morath to start a family as evidence that Monroe was out of his system. It was an insult to her to see him moving on with his life as if she'd never existed.

Her depression was compounded by the fact that Sinatra announced his engagement to Juliet Prowse in the second week of January. She hadn't seen this coming. News on the career front was bad too. Her fan mail dipped from 8000 letters a day to just 50 a week. Newspapers reported that her fame might be on the skids. A film poll listing the top stars of the day didn't even have her among the top 25. This was probably due to the fact that *Let's Make Love* and *The Misfits* had both misfired at the box office.[2]

Greenson saw her going downhill. He suggested she buy a house. His thinking was that it might act as a substitute to her for not having a husband or child.[3]

She didn't think she was beautiful anymore. If her looks went, she thought, what was left? When Montgomery Clift lost his chocolate box handsomeness, she said, he was still able to turn in fantastic performances. She didn't think she'd be able to as her crow's feet increased: "When my face goes, my body goes. I'll be nothing."[4]

She said to Lena Pepitone, "Nobody's ever gonna marry me now. I can't have kids. I can't cook. I've been divorced three times. Who would want me?"[5]

The house was situated on Helena Drive, a cul-de-sac off Sunset Boulevard. The fact that it was on a dead end seemed symbolic. A motto above the door said "Cursum Perficio." Translated into English it meant, "I've finished my race."[6] Never was a residence more aptly named. She described it as a "fortress where I can feel safe from the world."[7]

She bought it for $77,500, paying half in cash and taking out a mortgage for the remainder.

She might have expected to be well off financially at this stage because of her earnings from *Some Like It Hot* and *The Misfits* but high earnings can sometimes be as much of a curse as a blessing, at least as far as the IRS is concerned. She was now in the 90 percent tax bracket.

Greenson believed buying the house would help her shed her feelings of being orphaned all those years ago but instead it only compounded her sense of loneliness.

In many ways the house resembled the one Eli Wallach owned in *The Misfits*. It was unfinished in the same way his was, and for similar reasons. Her mind was in flux.

She tried to give it a personal touch by buying furniture for it but much of this sat in boxes and was unpacked. She told Sinatra that she was missing Hugo, the basset hound she'd had in Roxbury. He gave her a French poodle to act as a substitute. She called it Maf. That was her short term for Mafia, a tease at Sinatra's Mob connections. Sinatra hated the name, not only because it brought up a subject he was sensitive about but also because it was inappropriate. "Why not Fifi or Pierre?" he asked. "You know, something French."[8] But Monroe wouldn't be swayed.

A woman called Eunice Murray moved in with her. She was a housekeeper provided by Greenson. She was supposed to double as a nurse even though she had no medical background.

Murray's husband had deserted her years before. Eventually they became divorced. After her sister died she married her widower, her brother-in-law. Then *he* died. She'd got to know Greenson after selling her house to him. Afterwards he employed her as a nursemaid to many of his children. To Monroe she took on the role of a surrogate mother. One of her own daughters was actually called Marilyn.

As well as being her nursemaid, Murray chauffeured Monroe around Los Angeles. She also did her cooking and cleaning. As was the case with Greenson, the multi-tasking gave her far too much control over her life.

In time Murray became more a plant of Greenson's than anything else. Monroe's revelations to her were transmitted to him for him to interpret. She had a kind of psychological power over her that ill-befitted her status. It was even evident in the way they addressed one another. Murray called Monroe "Marilyn" whereas Monroe addressed Murray as "Mrs. Murray." She was as forbidding a figure as Mrs. Danvers in *Rebecca*.[9]

In essence Greenson had sent her to Monroe to act as a spy, reporting back to him on who she was seeing. Monroe's hairdresser George Masters described her as being "like a witch, terrifying. She was terrifically jealous of Marilyn, separating her from her friends."[10]

Murray objected to being called Monroe's housekeeper, insisting she was much more than that – chauffeur, real estate agent, social secretary and friend.[11] She left out the bit about tabulating all her behavior patterns and reporting them back to Greenson. Monroe found her "creepy."[12]

On February 19 Monroe went to Mexico. She said she was going to buy more furniture for her new home but she may also have been thinking of adopting a child. Her house reminded her of the orphanages she'd spent so much time in when she was growing up. She didn't say why. It was unusual for her to mention this as a positive aspect of it.[13] She had a brief romance with a screenwriter called Jose Bolanos while she was there and also visited an orphanage, giving a generous donation to it. If she was considering adopting a child, she dropped the idea. That might have been because there was no man in her life now. She believed a child needed two parents.[14]

Susan Strasberg thought she was more in love with the idea of children than children themselves: "She'd seemed frightened holding a friend's infant, as if the reality intruded on her fantasy." Strasberg found it strange hearing her talk about being a mother when she was such a child herself.[15]

Her thoughts went back to her career. She considered appearing in *Rain*, a TV adaptation of Somerset Maugham's short story about a woman of easy virtue, Sadie Thompson, being confronted by a fire-and-brimstone preacher. She was also considering two films

Sinatra mentioned to her, *Born Yesterday* and *How to Murder Your Wife*.

*Rain* had previously been filmed twice, in 1928 with Joan Crawford and in 1953 with Rita Hayworth. Lee Strasberg felt Monroe would be a good fit for the character of Thompson. She had similar problems with drink and drugs as Monroe had. (They would also both die at the same age – 36.) The idea of being seen as a sexual object seemed cut out of her own life too.

She'd been slated to sign her contract for *Rain* the previous year. She hadn't been able to because of going to Payne-Whitney. The project rumbled on for some months before eventually being abandoned. Everyone was disappointed, including Maugham himself. He thought she'd have been wonderful in the role.

She was also considering John Huston's *Freud*, in which Montgomery Clift would be playing the famous psychiatrist. Despite all Huston had gone through with her in *The Misfits*, he didn't rule her out. She passed on it, however, being in the middle of psychiatric treatment at the time, an irony that wasn't lost on some of her commentators.[16]

She would have been playing one of Freud's patients in the film. Greenson disapproved and so did Anna Freud, Sigmund's daughter, who, as mentioned, was friendly with Marianne Kris. Another prospect was a film called *Goodbye Charlie* in which a man is reincarnated as a woman. She'd been offered this while on the set of *The Misfits*. Clark Gable was amused when she mentioned it to him. "You don't have that kind of equipment!" he laughed.[17]

*Freud* would have been her preference of all of these if other things were equal. Jean-Paul Sartre even wanted her for it. The disapproval of Anna Freud overrode his enthusiasm.[18]

In the end she signed for *Something's Got to Give*, a title that proved to be grimly prophetic. It was a remake of the 1940 comedy *My Favorite Wife* with Cary Grant and Irene Dunne. The plot concerns a woman who's believed to have drowned years before. When she turns up, her husband is about to re-marry. She didn't like the director, Frank Tashlin, and had him replaced with George Cukor. Despite her problems on *Let's Make Love*, she valued Cukor. He'd put up with her tantrums more often than not.

As soon as shooting began she came down with a severe case of sinusitis. She also had a fever from a bug she'd caught in Mexico. Doctors suggested delaying the start of the film but studio executives wouldn't agree to that. They thought she was faking illness. She wanted filming to start late in the morning as it had on *The Misfits* but this was ruled out too. She was expected to be on the set at seven. That meant getting up at five.

Cukor had the same problems with her undermining his direction as Huston had on *The Misfits*. After each take she deferred to Paula Strasberg to approve it before she was happy. They had serious discussions together. Cukor felt these were all wrong for the film: "It was a comedy. They didn't fit."[19]

*Something's Got to Give* was a step backwards for Monroe, a return to the kind of caper she'd been making before she'd started to take herself seriously. She realized early on that it didn't have much to offer her. On *Let's Make Love* she was able to complain to Miller in the evenings about the dreadfulness of the script. She even prevailed on him to re-write some of it. Here there was nobody to confer with. Her loyal club of devotees from *The Misfits* were missing. There was nobody to sympathize with her but her costar Dean Martin, but they hadn't shared any scenes before her disenchantment set in.

Monroe continued to be late or absent. Cukor wasn't able to handle it anymore. He started tearing out what remained of his hair. He also started to chew the edges of the script. Tony Randall, another member of the cast, noticed his mouth white from the paper.

She was absent from the set more often than present. Some of the crew members joked that the first time they saw her was the last time. On one of the few days she showed up she stripped naked. It was for a swimming pool scene. It was as if she was reverting back to the young woman who'd done *Playboy*, the one who'd relished the idea of a street ventilator blowing the pleats of her dress above her knees as dozens of people looked on during shooting of *The Seven Year Itch*. Out of the 36 days of filming she only appeared on twelve. On many of these she was late. Cukor had no more than seven minutes of usable film to show for all that time.

Nudity in films may be commonplace today but in 1962 it was rare. When Miller saw the swimming pool footage he despaired. It was a betrayal of everything he'd aspired to for Monroe - and everything she'd aspired to for herself. He'd written *The Misfits* for her to give her a chance to outgrow the sex symbol tag. Wasn't this what she spent so much time agonizing over in their marriage? Wasn't it the reason she balked at *Some Like It Hot* and so many other films before it? Now she was throwing them all to the wind, returning to the sexploitative image she'd started out with. Maybe he shouldn't have been surprised. Her wish to have her breast exposed in the breakfast scene with Gable in *The Misfits* showed nothing really had changed. By now Fox had poured over $2 million into the film with precious little to show for it.

One of the reasons for Monroe's absenteeism on the set was a birthday party for John F Kennedy that she attended in May in Madison Square Garden. She was advised not to go because she'd told Cukor she was ill at the time. She sang "Happy Birthday" to Kennedy at the party. Peter Lawford introduced her as "the late Marilyn Monroe." That seemed fitting – and ominous. Also fitting was the fact that she sang it to the air of "Thanks for the Memory." That's all Kennedy would soon be to her – a memory.

Monroe didn't look well on the night. She seemed exhausted. Her hair was so lacquered it had no life in it. She was sewn into her dress so tightly it was as if the seamstress had forgotten to say "When."

Kennedy enjoyed her rendition. It was so sweet and wholesome, he said, he could now "retire from politics."[20]

"Sweet" and "wholesome" were hardly the words to describe her delivery. If anything, it was like an invitation for him to celebrate it in her boudoir.

Dorothy Kilgallen wrote in her newspaper column the following day that Monroe seemed to be making love to Kennedy – in front of four million people. If he had any intention of continuing a relationship with her, they were scuppered that night. She was a luxury he couldn't afford.[21]

GableMonroe Clift in The John Huston Production the Misfits Thelma Ritter Eli Wallach Arthur Miller Frank E. Taylor John Huston

*Monroe showed such energy when she was motivated It's difficult to believe she had such a short time to live.*

Why had she done it? Was it from loneliness? Desperation? The need to show Miller she was still sexy? This, after all, was one thing she would always have over Morath. Morath had accompanied Miller to a state dinner with Jackie Kennedy the previous week. It was almost like, "Anything you can do I can do better."

Monroe celebrated her 36th birthday when she got back to the set. The Greensons gave her an unusual gift: a champagne glass with her name engraved inside. She quipped, "Now I'll know who I am when I'm drinking."[22]

Evelyn Moriarty, her stand-in, bought the cake. It had "Happy Birthday (Suit)" written on it, a reference to her nude swimming scene. Cukor wasn't pleased. He refused to let the festivities begin until the day's shooting was completed. Too much time had been lost already. Nobody knew it then but this would be her last day on a film set. That night she went to a baseball game that was being played for the Muscular Dystrophy Association. She threw the opening ball. It was a chilly night and she caught a cold. It prevented her from returning to work on the next shooting day.

She didn't want to miss the game because she'd promised to bring Dean Martin's son to it.

Another day of shooting was lost. They let her know it in no uncertain terms. She felt the top brass were closing in. "They wanted me out," she said, "I could tell.[23]

She played brinkmanship with the studio bosses and eventually their patience with her ran out. There was one too many no-shows. She was fired at the beginning of June for "persistent absenteeism."[24]

Fox wasn't doing well financially at this point. *Cleopatra*, which netted Elizabeth Taylor $1 million, had cost $25 million to make. It nearly bankrupted the studio. Monroe picked a bad time to be difficult. She'd gotten away with unpunctuality with Billy Wilder and Huston. This was different.

Wilder once said, "I have an aunt in Vienna who would be on the set every morning at six and would know her lines backwards. But who would go to see her?"[25] His enthusiasm wasn't shared by Cukor. No longer was Marilyn Monroe Fox's prized commodity anymore. Elizabeth Taylor was.

After being fired, an action was put in place to sue her for pushing up the cost of the film. She was a lamb sacrificed on the burnt altar of the studio's epic fail with *Cleopatra*. Her salary for *Something's Got to Give* was $100,000, a tenth of what Taylor was getting.

"It's not fair," Monroe groaned. "Why don't they ever blame her?"[26] They'd always been rivals. A mutual friendship with Clift intensified the situation. Richard Burton once said to Taylor, "You like me but you *love* Monty."

The shutdown of *Something's Got to Give* was significantly different to that of *The Misfits*. On that occasion it was a joint decision. Here it was imposed on her. Neither had she a financial stake in *Something's Got to Give*, or any involvement in its circulation. It was out of her hands in all senses.

Over 100 jobs were lost as a result of these events. Not surprisingly, a lot of anger was directed at Monroe as a result, not only by the cast of the film but the crew members as well.

It was their anger that hurt her most of all. She'd always had a particular bond with them on film sets. Now she was being accused of betraying them. She thought this was unfair. She hadn't stormed off the set in a rage. She was genuinely ill for many of the days she was absent. She thought Cukor could have shot around her on at least some of those days. She felt more sinned against than sinning. It was an ignominy to be fired from a studio at which she'd worked for sixteen years. She was treated like a diva looking for attention instead of a troubled woman on her last nerve. A therapist should have been called in rather than lawyers.

Greenson assured the studio heads Monroe would be able to finish the film. He'd pulled her through *The Misfits*, he told them. He'd get her through this film too.

She couldn't believe what was happening. It would have been inconceivable to think of Monroe being fired from a film like *Some Like it Hot* despite what she put Billy Wilder through. It would have been equally inconceivable to think of her being fired from *The Misfits*. How could Huston have done it? Or United Artists? She was surrounded by too many members of her "fan club." Not to mention a husband, alienated and all as he was. These films were also well on the road when she started developing problems. *Something's Got to Give* was different. She had no gofers around to help her. Instead she lay marooned on the island of her demons, a reed blowing in the wind. Too few scenes had been shot to render her indispensable.

The industry was changing. Checkbooks ruled now. Her fame counted for nothing in the new regime. Reputations were re-negotiated on a daily basis.

She was replaced by Lee Remick. They were roughly the same size. Her costumes wouldn't have to be re-designed. The cameras could start rolling again.

Or could they? Martin was having none of it. "I have the greatest respect for Miss Lee Remick and her talent," he said, "but I signed to do the picture with Marilyn Monroe and I'll do it with no one else."[27] An action was filed by the studio against him. He threatened to countersue. So did Monroe. A stand-off resulted. Once again the absent actress was calling the shots.

Apart from everything else, Martin didn't think Remick was right for the film. The plot has him leaving Cyd Charisse for Monroe. He didn't think audiences would believe he'd have left her for Remick.[28]

By now the situation had become so messy that negotiations were put in place at the end of June to have Monroe reinstated. In July she met the studio chiefs at Twentieth Century-Fox to help expedite this. At the beginning of August it drafted up a new contract for her. There were even added perks.

She agreed to return to the film. Everything sounded ideal - but it wasn't. Her heart wasn't in it anymore. The fact that they'd fired her stuck more in her mind than the enhanced contract. It was too little too late. Suddenly she didn't care anymore.

She didn't care about the films or about life itself. Too much had happened. The impressionable young girl who'd burst on the scene as a breath of fresh air all those years ago had been pummeled too much. The failed marriages, the abortions, the miscarriages, the indignities, the substance abuse – all these things piled up in her head, making her feel like it was going to explode.

More than anything else she was resentful of the upswing in Miller's fortunes. It was in such marked contrast to her own. He had a screenwriting career up and running as well as a new partner. And a forthcoming child. All Monroe had was a string of

*Monroe having her hair styled as Paula Strasberg and a partially obscured Miller look on.*

departed lovers. All she had was a career she was hanging onto by the skin of her teeth. She was losing her face and her figure. She was at the tender mercies of lawyers to keep her in work.

Such must have been her thoughts as she lay on her bed in Helena Drive on the last day of her life.

On August 4, the fifth anniversary of the death of the baby she'd lost with Miller, she had a six hour consultation with Greenson. She took an overdose of Nembutal that night. There had been many of these before. Usually there was someone on hand to rescue her on these occasions, or even someone on the end of a phone line. This time there wasn't.

The overdose proved to be fatal. Marilyn was gone.

As the life ebbed out of her, a phonograph needle scratched on a record player. She had been playing, what else, a Frank Sinatra song. In 1958 she'd written a poem which contained the lines, "Help Help/Help I feel life coming closer/When all I want is to die.[29] Now it was even closer.

Images of her body being carried out of her house on a stretcher stunned people. The house itself looked tacky. It wasn't what her fans expected from the star who was once Twentieth Century-Fox's most prized acquisition. Tousled sheets, dowdy walls, unpacked boxes...it might have been the living quarters of a fifth rate star, even an extra.

At 9 a.m. an ambulance drove her body to the coroner's office. The autopsy was completed by 10.30 a.m. Afterwards it lay unclaimed on a slab in the storage vault. She was Case Number 81228. Graham McCann wrote, "Monroe dead had no one to claim her, her life ending as it began."[30]

She'd become a piece of meat like the wild horses in *The Misfits*, reverting to being Norma Jean Baker again, an unknown person. The envelope pattern was even reflected in her birth and death dates. She lived from 1926 to 1962, a direct inversion of the same numbers.

"I always felt I was a nobody," she said once. "The only way for me to be a somebody was to be somebody else."[31] That was why she became an actress in the first place. "The higher she climbed," Sidney Skolsky reflected "the more lost she became like Hemingway's leopard on Mount Kilimanjaro."[32] "I started with nothing," she once predicted, "and I'm going to end with nothing."[33] How right she was.

The woman desired by almost every full-blooded man in America died alone. Someone with an entourage that could minister to her every need at the flick of a button was, at the end, unable to contact any of them.

She'd made a number of phone calls before she became unconscious. Nobody was quite sure who they were to. Had she been trying to reach Sinatra? DiMaggio? Miller? What about the Kennedys? She had Jack's private number in the White House.[34] The last voice she heard, according to one of her biographers, was probably that of an operator informing her that Ralph Roberts was out for the evening.[35]

Investigations began into what exactly happened on the night. Eunice Murray said she saw her light on in the middle of the night, that a phone cable trailed under her door.

The sight of the cord concerned her more than the light. Monroe always put the phone in an adjoining room before going to sleep. She was a light sleeper and hated being woken up by it.

She lived for a number of hours after taking the Nembutal. If her phone calls were cries for help, they weren't picked up on. Maybe she'd cried wolf once too often. People had stopped hearing her. How many people did she call? How many answered? Nobody will ever know for sure. The phone records, like so many other items of interest that night, went AWOL.

A recording of her voice on one of the calls survived. It was to Peter Lawford, the man who set her up with the Kennedys. She said, "Say goodbye to Pat. Say goodbye to Jack. And say goodbye to yourself, because you're a nice guy."[36] Pat was Lawford's wife. Jack was Jack Kennedy, the man who'd referred to her as "the late Marilyn Monroe" so recently. Now his words were coming home to roost.

"I know I have to die," she said to Susan Strasberg one day, "but I hope I don't have to get old and sick to do it."[37] She believed she was never going to be long for the world but it remains a matter of conjecture whether she intended that night to be her last or not.

Either way she was a victim of a life that always seemed to be running away from her. It demanded she relinquish more and more of herself to the amphetamines that, in the end, dominated it.

Greenson became the target of much abuse in the aftermath of her demise. It was he, after all, who wrote her prescriptions. He defended himself by saying he gave her as many pills as she asked for to prevent her looking for them elsewhere. He knew she could – and would – do this if she didn't get what she wanted from him. Was he protesting too much or making a valid point about damage limitation? Similar questions would be asked about Elvis Presley's Dr Nichopoulos after Presley died from a lethal cocktail of barbiturates fifteen years later.[38]

Both Huston and Wallach believed her death was accidental. They thought she mixed up her medicines. Miller had a more complex attitude: "She was always playing with suicide. She was trying to get as close as she could [but] I always thought it was an accident. I can't believe she went over voluntarily. She needed a little luck to keep her [alive] that day." As to the question of whether he could have saved her, he said, "No." How could he when all the professionals failed? "I had the illusion," he said, "that if I didn't take care of her she'd come to a catastrophic end because she was living on the edge of her acceptance of life."[39] Huston said the cries he heard from her on the set of *The Misfits* were like responses to "the brutal violations of her life."[40] He'd directed her in her first major film and her last one. He never became intimate with her but he presided over the cycle of her fame from orphan child to icon to femme fatale.

Miller didn't go to her funeral. What would have been the point? "She won't be there."[41]

In later years he added, "To join what I knew would be a circus of cameras and shouts and luridness was beyond my strength. To me it was meaningless to stand for photographs at a stone."[42]

His letters were found among her possessions. Despite crossing him out of photographs of her and giving people to believe she'd cut him out of her life, she'd kept these. Why? Was there something about him she didn't want to let go? Would she even have admitted that to herself? Most of the letters were romantic. They capture aspects of their relationship at a time when it was going well, when the prospect of them finding happiness together was very real. Maybe she needed to return to that time to make her feel there was some reason to go on living. Maybe she thought she could repeat it with someone else.

Miller wasn't the only one of her inner circle who didn't attend her funeral. Sinatra didn't go either, nor Peter Lawford. They didn't give reasons. People who spoke to her close to the end had too much to lose by being seen there. Not too long before, Monroe had stayed away from Clark Gable's funeral from a combination of guilt and shame. Now it was other people's turn.

Her reputation continued to rise after her death. Like James Dean seven years before, she became almost beatified for many. She was seen as a fawn in the jungle of film-making, a candle in the wind of bureaucracy. Hollywood, she had said once, was a place that offered you "a thousand dollars for a kiss and fifty cents for your soul."[43]

Billy Wilder saw it the other way around. Hollywood didn't kill Monroe, he said. It was the Marilyn Monroes who were killing Hollywood.[44]

When the dust settled, some perspective was achieved. She was beautiful but flawed, adorable but of limited talent, heavenly on screen but impossible to live with.

The films she criticized, like *The Misfits* and *Some Like It Hot*, were the ones she was most remembered for. Those she spoke well of – *Don't Bother to Knock* and *The Asphalt Jungle* – were largely forgotten. *The Misfits*, it was generally agreed, showed that beneath the sex symbol lurked a human being whose hopes and fears "weren't altogether unlike those of a man."[45] Frank Taylor called it her spiritual autobiography.[46]

Was it fame or pills that killed her? One, of course, led to the other. In her last interview she said fame stirred up envy. People felt it gave them "some kind of privilege to walk up to you and say anything and it won't hurt your feelings. It's like it's happening to your clothing."[47]

She was buried in her *Misfits* wig.[48] Lee Strasberg gave the oration at the funeral. She left 60 percent of her estate to him as

well as the rights to *The Prince and the Showgirl*. May Reis was bequeathed $50,000.[50]

Monies weren't disbursed to these or other beneficiaries for nearly a decade because of legal obstacles. Strasberg's second wife, who never met Monroe, ended up getting the money. She also earned a fortune on royalties that had accumulated during that time.

The images from *Something's Got to Give* where she swam naked in the swimming pool were sold to Hugh Hefner for $25,000. Global sales brought the overall price to $150,000. The man who'd photographed her for *Playboy* in 1949 got $200. Monroe earned $50 for the centerfold.

There were many books written about her in the following years. Never one to miss an opportunity to do her down, Billy Wilder quipped, "There have been more books on Marilyn Monroe than on World War II – and there's a great similarity between them."[51]

One of the most controversial was Norman Mailer's *Marilyn* in 1973. Mailer and Miller shared a brownstone together at the end of the forties. Mailer was working on *The Naked and the Dead* then and Miller on *Death of a Salesman*. They would both become nationally famous very soon but they didn't share much except a few words with one another whenever they passed on the stairs. Mailer also lived near Miller and Monroe when they were in their Roxbury house. He fantasized about meeting Monroe. "I would have tried to make her fall in love with me," he said; "I would have thought of writing a play in which she'd star."[52]

His biography of her was originally supposed to be just a 25,000 word preface to a book of photographs of her. He took on the project half-heartedly but then became consumed by it. The resulting book was part novel and part biography. It became more Mailer than Monroe in the end as his penchant for "factoids" (his term for mixing fact and fiction) took over. His book was an attempt to appropriate Monroe for himself in print when he couldn't do so in reality.[53]

He continued to be obsessed with her all his life, even to the extent of linking their names together. "Norma" Miller was almost an anagram of Norman Mailer. So was Marilyn Monroe. Mailer always wanted to be invited around to their home but it didn't happen. He wasn't the type of man who appealed to Monroe. She didn't like his writing and she regarded his personality as too overpowering. Besides, one writer in the family was enough. Miller feared he'd try to seduce her so he didn't encourage any visits from him either.

He wrote of her at one point, "Marilyn was every man's love affair with America. She was blonde and beautiful and she had a sweet

*Monroe is seen here in one of her familiar scenes of emotional wreckage.*
*Miller tapped into that side of her for Roslyn but for Monroe it was too close*
*to the bone and she resented him for it.*

little rinky-dink of a voice and all the cleanliness of all the clean
American backyards. She was our angel, the sweet angel of sex.
The sugar of sex came up from her like a resonance of sound in the
clearest grain of a violin."[54]

People love conspiracy theories. There were many of these in the
years following her death. She was said to have been murdered by

the Mafia, the CIA, the Kennedys, even Greenson. Paper doesn't refuse ink and some of these theories are still being pedaled today in various configurations to sell magazines.

One of them suggested the Strasbergs had a hand in her death. According to this line of "reasoning" they'd heard she was going to change her will, which listed them as the main beneficiaries, and arranged to have her killed before she could do so. This theory becomes even more ludicrous in light of the fact that she was practically broke when she died.

One of the more fanciful theories concerning her death intimated she was killed by an enema. This isn't as ridiculous as it sounds because there was no water glass found in her bedroom on the night of her death. How did she consume so many Nembutals without one?

Her claim during her final year that she was under surveillance by the FBI gained some credence in 1977 when a man repairing the roof of her house fell through it and landed on some rusted relay transmitters.[55]

For years after her death, DiMaggio sent six red roses to her crypt three times a week.[56] She once said the camera was her only true lover.[57] If that was true, he ran it a close second.

Everyone had a theory on why she died. Kenneth Anger thought it resulted from the fact that the fiefdom that created her had lost too much money from "the wool-headed queen" because of her repeated tardiness.[58] Marlon Brando said she died because she stopped believing the "ballyhoo and hype" about her: "Her life was elsewhere."[59]

John Kobal wrote, "Nobody could project so much vitality for so long without finally paying the price."[60] Henry Hathaway contended, "You don't have to hold an inquest to find out who killed her. It was those bastards in the executive chairs.[61]

*James Barton, Gable and a would-be mustanger slake their thirst in the Reno bar.*

# Aftermath

Miller's child was born the year Monroe died. It was a girl. He named her Rebecca. Maybe it was better she wasn't there to witness the birth. He had another child the following year, Daniel. Daniel suffered from Down Syndrome. Miller was devastated.

He continued to put Monroe into his writings. She'd woken his muse with *The Misfits* after a fallow period. He continued to visit the wellspring of creativity in a manner that at times bordered on the voyeuristic. His play *After the Fall* is the most obvious example of this. It was his first full length play in eight years.

Helen Rowland said that love was a quest, marriage a conquest and divorce an inquest.[1] The last part of that epigram applied literally to *After the Fall*. It forensically ripped apart his relationship with Monroe in a way that made *The Misfits* look like a fairytale.

He made the two main characters into a singer and a lawyer rather than an actress and a writer but nobody was fooled about its origins. He said Morath encouraged him to write it in order to exorcise Monroe's ghost. In doing that he would "set their marriage free."[2]

Quentin, the male lead, spends his time ruminating on his three wives. He divorces the first and loses the second to suicide. This is Maggie. She appears in an ash blonde wig like the one Monroe wore in *The Misfits*. She's sewn into skintight dresses. She speaks in Monroe's childlike voice – and wiggles like her when she walks.

Many of Quentin's lines read like transcripts of comments Miller might have made to Monroe: "I'm putting in forty percent of my time on your problems."[3] "You want to die and I really don't know how to prevent it."[4] "You eat those pills to blind yourself."[5] "Barbiturates kill by suffocation."[6]

*After the Fall* is like a microscope of their life together. It's a play which purports to sympathize with her demons but in effect just unearths her spirit for literary gain and a plea for sympathy.

Between the lines he's saying "Poor me." It's a morbid excoriation of his deceased wife interspersed with humorless soliloquies on life and love. Whatever artistic merit they possess is undone by their long-windedness.

In one of the scenes Maggie reminds Quentin of when she found a note he once wrote that said, "The only one I will ever love is my daughter."[7] This seems to be lifted directly from the incident in London where Monroe found his diary entry lying open on a table, presumably left there for her to read. It was the first major crisis in their marriage.

As well as being a tirade against Monroe, the play is an autopsy of a failed marriage. Miller doesn't come out of it unscathed. Monroe's character castigates him for being cold and sexually unresponsive, caring only about money and his work. To that extent Miller sees the mote in his own eye too.

It opened in New York in 1964. The director was Elia Kazan. It made more money for Miller than anything he'd done since *Death of a Salesman* but was deservedly pilloried for its bad taste. He said it was no more autobiographical than any of his other works, a laughable claim. The man who hadn't gone to her funeral because he wanted to avoid a media circus was now digging up her remains for a whole new generation to dissect – and raking in a fortune in the process.

The man who'd refused to "name names" to HUAC all those years ago was now turning State's witness on his own dead wife.[8]

Most of the women in the play are flawed. The only pure one is Helga, a refugee from the concentration camps of World War II. It won't come as a surprise to anyone to learn she's modeled on Morath.[9]

Miller wasn't surprised he became a hate figure with the media after the play was staged. Coming so soon after Monroe's death he knew it "had to fail."[10]

According to author Radie Harris, Miller left a copy of *After the Fall* for Monroe to see on the desk of their suite in the Mapes Hotel when they were filming *The Misfits*.[11] If he did, it would have been to humiliate her in the same way he'd done when he'd left his diary for her to see in London when she was filming *The Prince and the Showgirl*.

Other people who'd been involved in *The Misfits* were more inclined to fly under the radar. Montgomery Clift followed the film with a ten minute performance in *Judgment at Nuremberg* which he did for nothing. It won him an Oscar nomination. It was Clift at his best. In that brief time he managed to epitomize all the trauma of a Jew who was sterilized in a concentration camp during World War II. This was Method acting at its finest, enhanced rather than lessened by the fact that he was going through the d.t.s from alcohol at the time. He used that to enhance his acting. A man visibly crumbles before us on the screen, straining to express himself in tortuous circumstances. The fact that he had difficulty remembering his lines made the performance more authentic.

He then did *Freud*, reuniting with John Huston who directed it. Sigmund Freud had homosexual tendencies. The character played by David McCallum in the film was gay too. The signs were there that Clift was starting to come out of the closet. On a visit to St. Clerans to discuss the script with Huston he even brought one of his boyfriends with him. Huston was shocked. He'd heard rumors about Clift's sexuality but thought they were just that. Now they were being confirmed by Clift himself. Huston demanded that the man not appear on the set of the film.

The casting of Clift proved to be a nightmare for Huston. Even in the short time since *The Misfits* his frame of mind had deteriorated dramatically. So had his eyesight. He was also confrontational about the script. Huston lost patience with him often and took to making fun of him. At one point he joked that he needed a Seeing Eye dog. A war of attrition developed between them. His co-star, Susannah York, took his side against Huston, making it a three-sided conflict.

The "honeymoon" between Huston and Clift on *The Misfits* turned into a nightmare on *Freud* just as his honeymoon with Monroe on *The Asphalt Jungle* disappeared on *The Misfits*. By now Clift's drink problem had gotten worse. So had his depression over his appearance. He was confrontational with Huston about the dialogue in the film and exhibited a masochistic streak in a scene that required him to climb a rope. The scars he developed on his hands as a result of this were considerably worse than the ones he got during the horse-roping scene in *The Misfits*.

As the production ground to a halt, lawyers started to become involved. If Monroe were alive she would have been amused. The negotiations were reminiscent of what happened on *Something's Got to Give*. There were suits and countersuits about who was responsible for the problems. These dragged Clift down further into his vortex of depression. Once an actor's career is annexed by lawyers, the creative germ is seriously endangered. This applied particularly to someone as sensitive as Clift.

Monroe's death took a lot out of him. It had often been joked that she was the only person in Hollywood in a worse state of health than he was. Now she was gone.

"Deaths always come in threes in show business," he said. First Gable, then Marilyn. Would he be next?[12]

*Freud* took so much out of him he didn't make another film for four years. That was *The Defector*, a low grade spy drama. His main reason in making it was to show the film industry he was medically sound. By now he'd had three operations for his cataracts and one for a hernia. Stories about his drinking going out of control further endangered his reputation.

He was desperate to get his career back on track. He expressed an interest in *Reflections in a Golden Eye*, yet another Huston film that was in the works. Based on Carson McCuller's gothic novel, it dealt with the tragedy of a gay military man. It would have been the role that removed all viewers' doubts about his sexuality.

He was uninsurable on *Reflections* until Elizabeth Taylor put her salary for the film as collateral for him. It was a gesture he appreciated deeply.

"I can't get a job," he told people, "but Elizabeth is my greatest friend. She keeps trying to help. Everyone else has deserted me."[13]

He never got to make *Reflections in a Golden Eye*, dying of a heart attack shortly before it was due to begin. He was living with his partner, Lorenzo James, at the time. Marlon Brando took the role instead.

*The Misfits* appeared on television the night before he died. Lorenzo came up to his bedroom and asked him if he wanted to see it. "Absolutely not!" he roared back at him. The next morning Lorenzo went to wake him but found the door locked. He thought this was odd as Clift never locked his door. Lorenzo ran down to the garden and got a ladder. He climbed the rungs and got in through the bedroom window. He then saw Clift dead in his bed. He was lying face up with his glasses on but no clothes. Both of his fists were clenched. There were no empty bottles or any evidence of substance abuse. He'd been trying hard to get in shape for *Reflections*.[14]

He was too young to die but anyone who knew him felt that it was only a matter of time because of his lifestyle. Like James Dean he'd been "a remarkable rocket which had stopped short in mid-trajectory, leaving behind nothing but questions."[15]

Would he have been better off to die in his car crash as Dean had done? In that way we could have preserved our image of him as an Adonis, someone who checked out at the height of his fame. He'd have become an icon like Dean instead of someone who stumbled on in mediocre movies and died as a pale reflection of himself.

He never quite attained the status of Dean, nor indeed of Monroe, who eclipsed both of them in the public imagination.

# Endnote

Nobody talked too much about *The Misfits* in the 1970's or 1980's. A new generation of actors sprang up, and a new way of making films. People who'd seen it when it came out either had a sentimental attachment to it or felt too much was made of it.

Miller published his autobiography, *Timebends*, in 1987. It was brilliantly written in a stream-of-consciousness style and filled in many of the details on behind-the-scenes problems between himself and Monroe that were absent from media reports of their relationship. He took responsibility for some of these but painted a picture of Monroe that was almost scary in its neuroticism.

He neglected to mention Yves Montand in the book. This was either because he didn't want to write about being cuckolded or his guilt over the cavalier manner in which he regarded their fling. Whatever the reason, it's a glaring omission in a book that suffers from excessive detail in most of its other respects.

He didn't mention his Down Syndrome child in the book either. To a producer friend of his he described Daniel as "mongoloid".[1] He was placed in an institution and lived there for the rest of his life. Morath visited him almost every week but Miller never did. In fact he never mentioned him to anyone in public nor in any of his writings. One wonders what Monroe would have made of all of this. She loved children, especially those with problems. She would have found much to empathize with in Daniel's lostness and the fact that he was placed in care. If she'd lived to see his birth it may have made her feel less envious of Miller, the man who appeared to have everything coming up roses for him as she breathed her last. Rebecca went on to marry a man called, coincidentally, Daniel. He was the Irish actor Daniel Day Lewis. She met him on the set of Miller's *The Crucible* when he was appearing in that.

Miller went on writing about Monroe. As well as *After the Fall* she was in later works like *Broken Glass* (1994) and *Mr. Peter's*

*Connections* (1999). Apart from Eli Wallach he was the last survivor of anyone central to *The Misfits*.

Wallach had an interesting experience in 2000 when he was attending the Golden Boot Awards at the Beverly Hilton Hotel. After the ceremony finished he was approached by Clark Gable's son. He'd never met him before. "My name is John Clark Gable," the boy said. "You made my dad's last film with him. Could you tell me a little about him?"[2]

John Clark had grown up without hearing too much about his father, knowing him only through the reports of others. Kay kept him away from the public eye as much as she could. She felt that was his best chance to be his own man.

Wallach asked him what he did for a living. He said he was a race car driver. Wallach said, "That must be an inherited trait. Your dad was car crazy." He told him about Gable's gull wing Mercedes and how he brought him for a spin in it one day on the set of *The Misfits* on Lake Placid. "As we drove," Wallach recalled, "he seemed to float above the dry lake bed. My shoulders were pinned back against the seat. I didn't dare look at the speedometer.[3]

He told him he danced with his mother one night on the set too. He hadn't known she was pregnant. When he found out he said to Gable, "Why did you let me jump around dancing like a madman with Kay if you knew she was pregnant?" Gable replied, "At her last pregnancy the doctor ordered bed rest for several months and she miscarried. I figured let her dance and have fun and see what happens."[4]

John Gable had two children, one of whom he named Clark James. Kay died in 1983. Six years later John Clark acted in a film, a low budget western called *Big Jim*. "My name definitely helped me get my foot in the door," he admitted. But *Big Jim* was nowhere near *The Misfits* in quality. It didn't even make it into movie theatres.[5]

Forty years after the film was made, people were still talking about it – and Miller still writing about it. He was 89 when he wrote his play *Finishing the Picture*. It dealt with the making of a film with a problematic main star. A kind of sequel to *After the Fall*, it left audiences wondering if he'd ever stop writing about the woman who made him a household name just as much as his writing. The syndrome afflicted Norman Mailer too. He wrote a play about her in 1998 called *Strawhead*. His daughter Kate played Monroe.

In 1999 the possessions Monroe left to Lee Strasberg were sold for $13 million at Christie's in New York. A dress she wore in *Let's Make Love* fetched $53,000. The designer Tommy Hilfiger paid a fortune for two pairs of jeans she'd worn in *The Misfits*. The sheath dress she'd worn at John F. Kennedy's birthday celebrations in Madison Square Garden went for almost a million dollars. The books she had in her library were sold in a lot for $600,000. One of them had a scrap of paper inside it with "He doesn't love me" scribbled on it. Did she mean Miller?[6]

*Finishing the Picture* has so many elements of Monroe in it, it's impossible not to view it against the backdrop of *The Misfits*. Miller wrote about her unpunctuality, her pill-popping, her phone calls to her analyst, even the forest fire that stalled the film in mid-shoot. As well as the character based on Monroe, there are others based on John Huston, Frank Taylor and Lee Strasberg.

If we put *Finishing the Picture* with *The Misfits* and *After the Fall* we have a trilogy of disenchantment from Miller, a theatrical post-mortem that perhaps makes too much special pleading for comfort, at least to Monroe devotees. Nobody denies how much he suffered at her hands but as the old saying goes, "A gentleman never tells." Both during her life and after it he used her for literary fodder. Picking her bones apart like all the other necrophiliacs who made money from her memory placed him in a very exploitative club.

His attitude to her hardened as the years went on. Speaking of her in 2001 he said, "I spent four years doing nothing except *The Misfits*. There was no gratitude. It just increased her contempt."[7]

He stayed with Morath and they had a happy marriage. She died in 2002 and Miller himself three years later. Wallach lived until 2014. Thelma Ritter had died in 1969.

The bare breast footage of Monroe that Huston refused to use from the breakfast scene with Gable was preserved by Frank Taylor's son. He kept it in a vault until 2018.[8] He released it in August of that year. If we put it with her *Playboy* centerfold and the swimming pool scene from *Something's Got to Give* it forms a kind of triptych. She always loved showing off her body from her earliest days as a magazine cover dollybird and that never changed. With Taylor's carefully preserved cameo, the wheel appeared to have come full circle.

# Cast and Crew

**Main cast**

Clark Gable. . . . . . . . . . . . . . . . . . (Gay Langland)
Marilyn Monroe . . . . . . . . . . . . . . .(Roslyn Taber)
Montgomery Clift . . . . . . . . . . . . . . (Perce Howland)
Thelma Ritter. . . . . . . . . . . . . . . . . (Isabelle Steers)
Eli Wallach . . . . . . . . . . . . . . . . . . . . . (Guido)

**Supporting Cast**

James Barton, Kevin McCarthy, Estelle Winwood

SCREENPLAY BY . . . . . . . . . . . . . . Arthur Miller
MUSIC COMPOSED AND CONDUCTED BY   Alex North
PRODUCER . . . . . . . . . . . . . . . . . Frank E. Taylor
DIRECTOR. . . . . . . . . . . . . . . . . . . .John Huston
DIRECTOR OF PHOTOGRAPHY . . Russel Metty, A.S.C.
ART DIRECTION . . Stephen Grimes and William Newberry
SET DIRECTION . . . . . . . . . . . . . Frank McKelvy
FILM EDITOR . . . . . . . . . . . George Tomasini, A.C.E
PRODUCTION MANAGER . . . . . . . . . .C.O. Erickson
SECOND UNIT DIRECTION . . . . . . . . . .Tom Shaw
SOUND RECORDING . Philip Mitchell and Charles Grensbach
SCRIPT SUPERVISION . . . . . . . . . . . . Angela Allen
SECOND UNIT PHOTOGRAPHY . . . Rex Wimpy, A.S.C.
ASSISANT DIRECTOR . . . . . . . . . . . . Carl Beringer
ASSISTANT TO THE PRODUCER . . . . . Edward Parone
MONROE'S COSTUMES BY. . . . . . . . . .Jean Louis
HAIR STYLING . . . . . Sydney Guilaroff & Agnes Flanagan
MAKE-UP. . . . . . . . . Allan Snyder, Frank Predoha S.M.A
and Frank Larue

# Notes

## From Story to Film

1. Christopher Bigsby, *Arthur Miller* (London: Phoenix, 2009), 602.
2. Fred Lawrence Guiles, *Legend: The Life and Death of Marilyn Monroe* (Lanham, MD: Scarborough House, 1991) 326.
3. Nina Pepitone and William Stadiem, *Marilyn Monroe Confidential* (New York: Pocket Books) 98.
4. Jeffrey Meyers, *The Genius and the Goddess* (London: Arrow, 2010) 182-3.
5. *Ibid.*, 181.
6. Pepitone and Stadiem, *Marilyn Monroe Confidential*, 103.
7. Taraborelli, *The Secret Life of Marilyn Monroe*, 332.
8. Marie Clayton, *Marilyn Monroe: Unseen Archives* (Bath: Parragon, 2005), 329.
9. McCann, *Marilyn Monroe*, 154.
10. Barbara Leaming, *Marilyn Monroe* (London: Orion, 2002) 289.
11. Lois Banner, *Marilyn: The Passion and the Paradox* (London: Bloomsbury, 2012) 323.
12. Churchwell, *The Many Lives of Marilyn Monroe*, 72-3.
13. Leaming, *Marilyn Monroe,* 367.
14. *Ibid.*, 287.
15. Weatherby, *Conversations with Marilyn*, 188.
16. Tony Curtis with Mark A. Vieira, *Some Like It Hot: Me, Marilyn and the Movie* (London: Virgin, 2009) 38.
17. Wolfe, *The Assassination of Marilyn Monroe*, 321.
18. Robert LaGuardia, *Monty: A Biography of Montgomery Clift* (New York: Avon, 1977) 219.
19. Weatherby, *Conversations with Marilyn*, 58.
20. Elia Kazan, *A Life* (New York: Doubleday, 1989) 540.
21. Slatzer, Robert F. *The Marilyn Files* (New York: Shapolsky, 1992), 75.
22. Ethan Mordden, *Movie Star: A Look at the Women who Made Hollywood* (New York: St. Martin's Press, 1983), 226.
23. David Shipman, ed., *Movie Talk: Who Said What About Whom in the Movie,* (London: Bloomsbury, 1988), 147.
24. Curtis with Vieira, *Some Like It Hot: Me, Marilyn and the Movie,* 38.
25. Weatherby, *Conversations with Marilyn*, 90.
26. Strasberg, *Marilyn and Me*, 233.
27. David Garfield, *A Player's Place: The Story of the Actors Studio* (New York: The Macmillan Company, 1958) 251.
28. Harold Clurman, *Lies Like Truth: Theatre Reviews and Essays* (New York: The Macmillan Company, 1958) 251.
29. Strasberg. *Marilyn & Me*, 233.

30. John Huston, *An Open Book* (New York: Alfred A. Knopf, 1980), 286-7.
31. Axel Madsen, *John Huston* (London: Robson, 1979), 98-9.
32. Steinman, *Marilyn: Norma Jeane*, 152.
33. James Goode, *The Making of The Misfits* (New York: Limelight, 1986), 200.
34. Eli Wallach, *The Good, The Bad and Me* (Orlando, F1: Harcourt Inc., 2005), 218.
35. Eve Arnold, *Marilyn Monroe: An Appreciation* (London: Hamish Hamilton, 1987) 87.
36. Arthur Miller and Serge Toubiana, *The Misfits: Story of a Shoot* (New York: Phaidon, 2011), 36.
37. *John Huston Papers*, Margaret Herrick Library, Caliornia.
38. Meyers, *The Genius and the Goddess*, 213.
39. Lawrence Grobel, *The Hustons: The Life and Times of a Hollywood Dynasty* (New York: Skyhorse Publishing, 2014), 478.
40. *Ibid.*, 479.
41. Arthur Miller, *Timebends: A Life* (London: Methuen, 1987), 462.
42. Pepitone and Stadiem, *Marilyn Monroe Confidential*, 176-7.
43. LaGuardia, *Monty*, 218.
44. Jon Bradshaw, *Dreams That Money Can Buy: The Tragic Life of Libby Holman* (New York: William Morrow & Co.), 324.
45. Bosworth, *Montgomery Clift*, 299.
46. *Ibid,* 310.
47. *Ibid,* 313.
48. Boze Hadleigh, *Hollywood Bitch* (London: Robson, 1999), 224.
49. LaGuardia, *Monty*, 223.
50. Miller and Toubiana, *The Misfits*, 33.
51. Fred Lawrence Guiles, *Norma Jean: The Life of Marilyn Monroe* (London: Granada, 1985), 244.
52. Goode, *The Making of the Misfits*, 23-4.
53. David Bret, *Clark Gable: Tormented Star* (London: Robson, 2007), 244.
54. Jane Ellen Wayne, *Gable's Women* (New York: Prentice Hall Press, 1987), 266.

**L.A. Interlude**

1. Yves Montand, *You See, I Haven't Forgotten* (London: Chatto & Windus, 1992) 305.
2. Charles Casillo, *Marilyn Monroe: The Private Life of a Public Icon* (New York: St Martin's Press, 2018), 157-8.
3. Montand, *You See, I Haven't Forgotten*, 320.
4. Alex Finlayson, *Plays* (London: Oberton Books, 1998), 85.
5. Miller, *Timebends*, 466.
6. Gottfried, *Arthur Miller*, 326-7.
7. *Ibid.*, 421.
8. Clayton, *Marilyn Monroe*, 296.
9. Wolfe, *The Assassination of Marilyn Monroe*, 417-8.
10. Grobel, *The Hustons*, 486.
11. Simone Signoret, *Nostalgia Isn't What It Used To Be* (New York: Penguin, 1979), 338.
12. *Ibid.*, 339.
13. Guus Luijters, ed., *Marilyn Monroe In Her Own Words* (London: Omnibus Press, 1990), 71.
14. Montand, *You See, I Haven't Forgotten*, 325.
15. McClelland, ed., *StarSpeak*, 197.
16. Goode, *The Making of The Misfits*, 128.
17. *Ici-Paris*, July 6, 1960.
18. *Paris-Match*, July 16, 1960.

19. Clayton, *Marilyn Monroe*, 302.
20. Nigel Cawthorne, *Sex Lives of the Hollywood Goddesses* (London: Prion, 1997), 255.
21. Clayton, *Marilyn Monroe*, 302.
22. Montand, *You See, I Haven't Forgotten*, 336.
23. *Ibid.*, 394.
24. *Ibid.*, 326.
25. *Ibid.*, 327.
26. Guiles, *Norma Jean*, 327.
27. Montand, *You See, I Haven't Forgotten*, 309.

**Arrival in Reno**
1. Haspiel, *Marilyn: The Ultimate Look at the Legend*, 175.
2. Gottfried, *Arthur Miller*, 332.
3. Strasberg, *Marilyn and Me*, 247.
4. Patricia Bosworth, *Montgomery Clift: A Biography* (New York: Limelight, 2001), 353.
5. Wolfe, *The Assassination of Marilyn Monroe*, 321.
6. Grant, ed., *Clark Gable In His Own Words*, 55.
7. Weatherby, *Conversations with Marilyn*, 67.
8. Grant, ed., *Clark Gable In His Own Words*, 59.
9. Jane Ellen Wayne, *Clark Gable: Portrait of a Misfit* (London: Robson, 1993), 280.
10. *Hollywood Citizen News*, November 9, 1954.
11. Wallach, *The Good, the Bad and Me*, 216.
12. Ibid., 208-10.
13. Summers, Goddess, 176.
14. Wallach, *The Good, The Bad and Me*, 211.
15. *Ibid.*, 214-5.
16. Wayne, *Clark Gable*, 281-2.
17. Wayne, *Gable's Women*, 267.
18. Wayne, *Clark Gable*, 281.

19. Susan Strasberg, *Bittersweet* (New York: Putnam's, 1980), 84.
20. Michael Schneider, *Marilyn's Last Sessions* (Edinburgh: Canongate, 2006), 83.
21. Bigsby, *Arthur Miller*, 621-2.
22. Leaming, *Marilyn Monroe*, 365.

**Shooting Begins**
1. Bigsby, *Arthur Miller*, 616.
2. Miller and Toubiana, *The Misfits*, 54.
3. Guiles, *Legend*, 379.
4. Miller and Toubiana, *The Misfits*, 383.
5. Guiles, *Norma Jean*, 270.
6. Weatherby, *Conversations with Marilyn*, 32.
7. Leonard Moss, *Arthur Miller*, (Boston: Twayne, 1980), 55.
8. Arnold, *Marilyn Monroe: An Appreciation*, 120.
9. Miller and Toubiana, *The Misfits*, 94.
10. Arnold, *Marilyn Monroe: An Appreciation*, 72.
11. Clayton, *Marilyn Monroe*, 277.
12. Norma Mailer, *Marilyn* (London: Virgin 2012), 245.
13. Carl E. Rollyson, *Marilyn Monroe: A Life of the Actress* (London: New England Library, 1990), 59.
14. Goode, *The Making of The Misfits*, 203.
15. McCann, *Marilyn Monroe*, 158.
16. Lesley Brill, *John Huston's Filmmaking* (Cambridge: Cambridge University Press, 1997), 80.
17. Wallach, *The Good, the Bad and Me*, 213.
18. *Ibid.*, 215.
19. This is an echo of Roslyn's earlier line to Isabel, "You could touch him but he wasn't there."

20. *Making the Misfits*, WNET and Channel 4, 2001.
21. *Ibid.*
22. *New York Times*, February 5, 1961.
23. *Cosmopolitan,* December 1960.
24. Wallach, *The Good, the Bad and Me*, 218.
25. Wayne, *Gable's Women*, 268.
26. Anthony Summers, *Goddess: The Secret Lives of Marilyn Monroe* (London: Orion, 1985), 259.
27. Good, *The Making of The Misfits*, 67.
28. Guiles, *Legend,* 390.
29. Wallach, *The Good, the Bad and Me*, 222.
30. Arnold, *Marilyn Monroe: An Appreciation*, 70.
31. Miller and Toubiana, *The Misfits*, 120.
32. Bigsby, *Arthur Miller*, 625-6.
33. Miller and Toubiana, *The Misfits*, 71.
34. Guiles, *Norma Jean*, 142.
35. *Ibid.*, 343.
36. *Ibid.*, frontispiece.
37. Miller, *Timebends*, 369.
38. Spoto, *Marilyn Monroe*, 480-1.
39. Wallach, *The Good, the Bad and Me*, 217.
40. Clayton, *Marilyn Monroe*, 303.
41. Wolfe, *The Assassination of Marilyn Monroe*, 43`.
42. *Harper's*, August 1958.

**Problems with Marilyn**
1. Michelle Morgan, *Marilyn Monroe* (London: Constable & Robinson, 2012), 284-5.
2. Madsen, John Huston, 186.
3. Wallach, *The Good, the Bad and Me*, 221.
4. Grant, ed., *Clark Gable In His Own Words*, 59.

5. Miller, *Timebends*, 171-2.
6. Weatherby, *Conversations with Marilyn*, 31.
7. LaGuardia, *Monty*, 219.
8. Steinem, *Marilyn*, 211.
9. Leaming, *Marilyn Monroe*, 211.
10. McClelland, ed., *StarSpeak*, 24.
11. Miller and Toubiana, *The Misfits*, 150.
12. Guiles, *Legend*, 316.
13. Grobel, *The Hustons*, 489.
14. *Ibid.*
15. Pepitone and Stadiem, *Marilyn Monroe Confidential*. 154.
16. McClelland, ed., *StarSpeak*, 193.
17. Hadleigh, *Hollywood Bitch*, 46.
18. Wayne, *Gable's Women*, 21.
19. Grobel, *The Hustons*, 495.
20. Arnold, *Marilyn Monroe: An Appreciation*, 87.
21. Guiles, *Norma Jean*, 288.
22. Mailer, *Marilyn*, 260.
23. Taraborelli, *The Secret Life of Marilyn Monroe*, 334.
24. Arnold, *Marilyn Monroe: An Appreciation,* 88.
25. Casillo, *Marilyn Monroe*, 173.
26. Guiles, *Norma Jean,* 294.

**Perce**
1. LaGuardia, *Monty,* 218.
2. John Parker, *Five for Hollywood* (New York: Carol Publishing, 1991), 186.
3. Barney Hoskyns, *Montgomery Clift: Beautiful Loser* (London: Bloomsbury, 1991), 166.
4. *Screen Stories*, February 1961.
5. Goode, *The Making of the Misfits*, 117.
6. Nolan, William F., *John Huston: King Rebel* (Los Angeles, CA: Sherbourne Press, 1965), 183.
7. Morgan, *Marilyn Monroe*, 288.

8. Wallach, *The Good, the Bad and Me*, 226.
9. Bosworth, *Montgomery Clift*, 356.
10. Nolan, *John Huston*, 185-6.

**Meltdown**

1. Wallach, *The Good, the Bad and Me*, 3.
2. Weatherby, *Conversations with Marilyn*, 53.
3. Strasberg, *Marilyn and Me*, 249.
4. Maurice Zolotow, *Billy Wilder in Hollywood* (New York: Limelight, 1996), 269.
5. Banner, *Marilyn*, 353.
6. Meyers, *The Genius and the Goddess*, 222.
7. Wallach, *The Good, the Bad and Me*, 225-6.
8. Norman Mailer, *Of Women and Their Elegance* (New York: Simon & Schuster, 1980), 145.
9. Miller, *Timebends*, 474.
10. *Ibid*, 475.
11. Guiles, *Norma Jean*, 286-7.
12. Summers, *Goddess*, 260-1.
13. Miller,.
14. Wolfe, *The Assassination of Marilyn Monroe*, 436.
15. Mailer, *Marilyn*, 255-6.
16. Summers, *Goddess*, 261.
17. *Ibid.*, 261-2.
18. Casillo, *The Private Life of a Public Icon*, 184-5.
19. Goode, *The Making of The Misfits*, 246-7.
20. Spoto, *Marilyn Monroe*, 488.
21. Miller, *Timebends*, 479-80.
22. John Kobal, *Marilyn Monroe: A Life on Film* (London: Hamlyn, 1974), 147-8.
23. Miller, *Timebends*, 481-2.
24. Nolan, *John Huston*, 190.
25. Miller and Toubiana, *The Misfits*, 26-7.
26. Grobel, *The Hustons*, 489-90.
27. Leaming, *Marilyn Monroe*, 371.
28. Wolfe, *The Assassination of Marilyn Monroe*, 385.
29. Strasberg, *Marilyn and Me*, 257.
30. Pepitone and Stadiem, *Marilyn Monroe Confidential*, 155.
31. *L.A. Mirror*, November 28, 1960.
32. Radie Harris, *Radie's New World* (New York: W.H. Allen, 1975, 195.
33. Wallach, *The Good, the Bad and Me*, 218.
34. *The Making of The Misfits*, WNET.
35. Patrick Agan, *The Decline and Fall of the Love Goddesses* (Los Angeles, Pinnacle, 1979), 281
36. Leonard, *Montgomery Clift*, 243.
37. Agan, *The Decline and Fall of the Love Goddesses*, 280
38. *L.A. Mirror*, August 26, 1960.
39. Guiles, *Norma Jean*, 131.
40. *L.A. Mirror*, August 26, 1960.
41. Miller and Toubiana, *The Misfits*, 147.
42. Gottfried, *Arthur Miller*, 32.
43. Grobel, *The Hustons*, 491.
44. Keith Badman, *The Final Years of Marilyn Monroe* (London: Aurum, 2012). 40.
45. Pepitone and Stadiem, *Marilyn Monroe Confidential*. 158.
46. Bosworth, *Montgomery Clift*, 354.
47. LaGuardia, *Monty*, 221.
48. Gabe Essoe, *The Complete Films of Clark Gable* (New York: Citadel Press, 1994), 253.
49. Parker, *Five for Hollywood*, 188.

**Last Scenes**

1. Wallach, *The Good, the Bad and Me*, 214.
2. Weatherby, *Conversations with Marilyn*, 53.
3. Nolan, *John Huston*, 185.

4. Goode, *The Making of The Misfits*, 150-1.
5. Huston, *An Open Book*, 290.
6. Michael Barson, *The Illustrated Who's Who of Hollywood Directors*, (New York: Farrar, Strais & Giroux, 1995), 211.
7. Jack Scagnetti, *The Life and Loves of Gable* (New York: Jonathan David, 1976), 152
8. Charles Samuels, *The King of Hollywood: A Biography of Clark Gable* (London: W.H. Allen, 1962), 219.
9. Nolan, *John Huston*, 189.
10. Spoto, *Marilyn Monroe*, 485-6.
11. Goode, *The Making of The Misfits*, 151.
12. Wayne, *Clark Gable's Women*, 273.
13. Barbara Walters Show, ABC-TV, November 6, 1991.
14. Spoto, *Marilyn Monroe*, 484-5.
15. Michael Freedland, *Gregory Peck* (New York: Morrow, 1980), 137-8.
16. Wallach, *The Good, the Bad and Me*, 219.
17. Miller and Toubiana, *The Misfits*, 13.
18. Morgan, *Marilyn Monroe*, 28.
19. Gottfried, *Arthur Miller*, 313.
20. Bigsby, *Arthur Miller*, 628.
21. Morgan, *Marilyn Monroe*, 288.
22. Arthur Miller, *Presence: Collected Stories* (London: Bloomsbury, 2010), 72.
23. Miller, *Presence*, 70.
24. *Ibid.*, 71.
25. *Ibid.*, 72
26. Rosemarie Jarski, ed., *Hollywood Wit* (London: Prion, 2000) 160.
27. Pepitone and Stadiem, *Marilyn Monroe Confidential*, 150.
28. *Ibid.*

29. Weatherby, *Conversations with Marilyn*, 54.
30. Banner, *Marilyn*, 429.
31. Leaming, *Marilyn Monroe*, 475.
32. Weatherby, *Conversations with Marilyn*, 54.
33. Bosworth, *Montgomery Clift*, 355.
34. Meyers, *The Genius and the Goddess*, 223.
35. Miller, *Timebends*, 485.
36. *Ibid.*, 474.
37. Weatherby, *Conversations with Marilyn*, 75.
38. *Ibid.*
39. Miller, *Timebends*, 466.
40. Goode, *The Making of The Misfits*, 77.
41. *Daily Telegraph*, October 10, 1987.
42. *Esquire*, February 3, 1961.

**Wrapping Up**
1. Goode, *The Making of The Misfits*, 201.
2. *Bozeman Chronicle*, January 23, 1961.
3. Cawthorne, *Sex Lives of the Hollywood Goddesses*, 257.
4. Arnold, *Marilyn Monroe: An Appreciation*, 93.
5. Summers, *Goddess*, 263-4.
6. Jack Cardiff, *Magic Hour: A Life in Movies* (London: Faber and Faber, 1997), 212.
7. Goode, *The Making of The Misfits*, 300.
8. Miller, *Timebends*, 485-6.
9. Grant, ed., *Clark Gable In His Own Words*, 61.
10. Nolan, *John Huston*, 190-1.
11. *L.A. Examiner*, January 29, 1961.
12. Leonard, *Montgomery Clift*, 245.
13. Clayton, *Marilyn Monroe*, 285.
14. Weatherby, *Conversations with Marilyn*, 97.

15. Goode, *The Making of The Misfits*, 248.
16. Casillo, *The Private Life of a Public Icon*, 176.
17. Samuels, *The King of Hollywood*, 219.
18. *Ibid.*, 215-6.
19. Bret, *Clark Gable*, 253.
20. *Ibid.*, 254.
21. Wayne, *Clark Gable*, 289.
22. Arnold, *Marilyn Monroe: An Appreciation*, 92.
23. Wayne, *Clark Gable*, 288.
24. *Ibid.*, 291.
25. Taraborelli, *The Secret Life of Marilyn Monroe*, 339.
26. *Ibid.*
27. Wayne, *Gable's Women*, 21.
28. Cawthorne, *Sex Lives of the Hollywood Goddesses*, 257.
29. Grobel, *The Hustons*, 499.
30. Wayne, *Clark Gable*, 290.
31. *Ibid.*, 290-1.
32. Spada, *Peter Lawford*, 332.
33. Badman, *The Final Days of Marilyn Monroe*, 43.
34. Wayne, *Clark Gable*, 292.
35. Nolan, *John Huston*, 191.
36. Samuels, *The King of Hollywood*, 21.

**Parting of the Ways**
1. Bigsby, *Arthur Miller*, 631.
2. *Ibid.*, 632.
3. Gottfried, *Arthur Miller*, 340.
4. Cardiff, *Magic Hour*, 212.
5. Summers, *Goddess*, 264.
6. *France-Dimanche*, November 16, 1960.
7. Gottfried, *Arthur Miller*, 337.
8. *Ibid.*
9. *New York Times*, November 12, 1960.
10. Mailer, *Marilyn*, 270.
11. Miller, *Timebends*, 521.

12. Summers, *Goddess*, 265.
13. Bigsby, *Arthur Miller*, 624.
14. Strasberg, *Marilyn and Me*, 200.
15. *Ibid.*, 256-7.
16. Bigsby, *Arthur Miller*, 633.
17. Summers, *Goddess*, 265.
18. *Cosmopolitan*, December 1960.
19. Leaming, *Marilyn Monroe*, 380.
20. Montand, *You See, I haven't Forgotten*, 333.
21. Miller, *Timebends*, 493.
22. Morgan, *Marilyn Monroe*, 318.
23. Spoto, *Marilyn Monroe*, 500.
24. Morgan, *Marilyn Monroe*, 297.
25. Schneider, *Marilyn's Last Sessions*, 132.
26. Spoto, *Marilyn and Me*, 504.
27. Strasberg, *Marilyn and Me*, 259.
28. McCann, *Marilyn Monroe*, 192.
29. Banner, *Marilyn*, 361.

**Reception and Fallout**
1. Gottfried, *Arthur Miller*, 339.
2. Bigsby, *Arthur Miller*, 629.
3. *Ibid.*, 635.
4. *New York Times*, February 2, 1961.
5. Essoe, *The Complete Films of Clark Gable*, 253.
6. Mailer, *Marilyn*, 251.
7. *Ibid.*, 204.
8. Marjorie Rosen, *Popcorn Venus: Women, Movies and the American Dream* (New York: Avon Books, 1973), 290.
9. Gottfried, *Arthur Miller*, 336.
10. Weatherby, *Conversations with Marilyn*, 161.
11. Barson, *The Illustrated Who's Who of Hollywood Directors*, 211.
12. *Esquire*, March 1961.
13. *Limelight Magazine*, February 9, 1961.
14. *Variety*, February 1, 1961.
15. Grobel, *The Hustons*, 493.

16. Miller and Toubiana, *The Misfits*, 30.
17. Goode, *The Making of The Misfits*, 87.
18. Moss, *Arthur Miller*, 56.
19. *New Yorker*, February 4, 1961.
20. Madsen, *John Huston*, 5.
21. Clayton, *Marilyn Monroe*, 302.
22. Badman, *The Final Days of Marilyn Monroe*, 43.
23. Summers, *Goddess*, 269-70.
24. Meyers, *The Genius and the Goddess*, 247.
25. Wolfe, *The Assassination of Marilyn Monroe*, 448-9.
26. *New York World Telegram*, February 10, 1961.
27. www.lettersofnote.com, July 19, 2010.
28. Schneider, *Marilyn's Last Sessions*, 374.
29. Badman, *The Final Days of Marilyn Monroe*, 41.
30. Monroe Letter to Greenson, March 2, 1961.
31. Wayne, *Clark Gable*, 291.
32. Badman, *The Final Days of Marilyn Monroe*, 26.
33. Wolfe, *The Assassination of Marilyn Monroe*, 460.
34. Kitty Kelley, *His Way: The Unauthorized Biography of Frank Sinatra* (New York: Bantam, 1987), 312.
35. Wolfe, *The Assassination of Marilyn Monroe*, 460.
36. John Austin, *Hollywood's Babylon Women* (New York: S.P.I. Books, 1994), 3.
37. Meyers, *The Genius and the Goddess*, 254.

**Goodbye Norma Jean**
1. Steinem, *Marilyn Monroe*, 155.
2. Wolfe, *The Assassination of Marilyn Monroe*, 96.
3. *The Legend of Marilyn Monroe*, CDA Entertainment Ltd., 2002.
4. Pepitone and Stadiem, *Marilyn Monroe Confidential*, 181.
5. Steinem, *Marilyn Monroe*, 107.
6. Schneider, *Marilyn's Last Sessions*, 333.
7. Guiles, *Legend*, 417.
8. Pepitone and Stadiem, *Marilyn Monroe Confidential*, 171.
9. Schneider, *Marilyn's Last Sessions*, 374.
10. Adam Victor, *The Marilyn Encyclopedia* (Woodstock, New York: Overlook Press, 1999), 209.
11. Badman, *The Final Days of Marilyn Monroe*, 55.
12. Pepitone and Stadiem, *Marilyn Monroe Confidential*, 217.
13. Morgan, *Marilyn Monroe*, 316-7.
14. Steinem, *Marilyn Monroe*, 53.
15. Strasbeg, *Marilyn and Me*, 156.
16. Parker, *Five for Hollywood*, 203.
17. Badman, *The Final Days of Marilyn Monroe*, 23.
18. Leonard, *Montgomery Clift*, 244.
19. Patrick McGilligan, *George Cukor: A Double Life* (London: Faber and Faber, 1992) 271.
20. Spada, *Peter Lawford*, 339.
21. Schneider, *Marilyn's Last Sessions*, 234.
22. Pepitone and Stadiem, *Marilyn Monroe Confidential*, 214.
23. Clayton, *Marilyn Monroe*, 378.
24. Shipman, ed., *Movie Talk*, 149.
25. Pepitone and Stadiem, *Marilyn Monroe Confidential*, 210.
26. Nick Tosches, *Dino: Living High in the Dirty Business of Dreams* (London: Minerva, 1993), 343-4.
27. Slatzer, *The Marilyn Files*, 95.

28. Schneider, *Marilyn's Last Sessions*, 166.
29. McCann, *Marilyn Monroe*, 52.
30. Rosemarie Jarski, ed., *The Funniest Things You Never Said 2* (London: Ebury Press, 2010), 381.
31. Summers, *Goddess*, 360.
32. Freeman, Lucy, *Why Norma Jeane Killed Marilyn Monroe* (New York: Hastings House, 1992), 7.
33. Lawford, *Peter Lawford*, 140.
34. Spoto, *Marilyn Monroe*, 335.
35. Meyers, *The Genius and the Goddess*, 262.
36. Strasbeg, *Marilyn and Me*, 231.
37. Nichopoulous' prescriptions were enhanced by extra ones discharged to his bodyguards under assumed names.
38. Bigsby, *Arthur Miller*, 634.
39. *The Legend of Marilyn Monroe*, CDA Entertainment Ltd., 2002.
40. Jarski, ed., *Hollywood Wit*, 167.
41. Gottfried, *Arthur Miller*, 347.
42. Luijters, ed., *Marilyn Monroe In Her Own Words*, 55.
43. Jarski, ed., *Hollywood Wit*, 167.
44. Barry Norman, *Talking Pictures* (London: Hodder & Stoughton, 1987), 98.
45. Miller and Toubiana, *The Misfits*, 184.
46. *Life*, August 3, 1962.
47. *The Many Lives of Marilyn Monroe*, DVD, 2001.
48. Wolfe, *The Assassination of Marilyn Monroe*, 66.
49. Arnold, *Marilyn Monroe: An Appreciation*, 91.
50. Meyers, *The Genius and the Goddess*, 197.
51. J. Michael Lennon, *Conversations with Norman Mailer* (Jackson, Mississippi: University Press of Mississippi, 2008), 203.
52. Churchwell, *The Many Lives of Marilyn Monroe*, 93.
53. Mailer, *Marilyn*, 1.
54. McCann, *Marilyn Monroe*, 186-7.
55. Peter Underwood, *Death in Hollywood* (London, Piatkus, 1992) 18.
56. Agan, *The Decline and Fall of the Hollywood Goddessess*, 283.
57. Kenneth Anger, *Hollywood Babylon* (London: Arrow, 1986), 279.
58. Stefan Kanfer, *Somebody: The Reckless Life and Remarkable Career of Marlon Brando* (London: Faber and Faber, 2008), 187.
59. John Kobal, *Marilyn Monroe: A Life on Film* (London: Hamlyn, 1974), 33.
60. Shipman, ed., *Movie Talk*, 147.
61. McCann, *Marilyn Monroe*, 169.

**Aftermath**

1. Jill Bauer, *From I Do to I'll Sue: An Irreverent Compendium For Survivors of Divorce* (London: Robson, 1994), 135.
2. Weatherby, *Conversations with Marilyn*, 219.
3. Arthur Miller, *After The Fall* (London: Penguin, 1992), 95.
4. *Ibid.*, 103.
5. *Ibid.*, 107.
6. *Ibid.*, 112.
7. *Ibid.*, 108.
8. Leaming, *Marilyn Monroe*, 430.
9. Banner, *Marilyn*, 430.
10. Miller, *Timebends*, 533.
11. Harris, *Radie's New World*, 195.
12. Bosworth, *Montgomery Clift*, 374.
13. *Ibid.*, 404.

14. *Ibid.*, 411-2.
15. Lancaster, *Montgomery Clift*, 30.

**Endnote**
1. Gottfried, *Arthur Miller*, 346.
2. Wallach, *The Good, The Bad and Me*, 228.
3. *Ibid.*
4. *Ibid.*, 229.
5. Wayne, *Clark Gable*, 292-3.
6. Schneider, *Marilyn's Last Sessions*, 352.
7. Bigsby, *Arthur Miller*, 644.
8. *Daily Telegraph*, August 12, 2018.

# Bibliography

Adams, Cindy, *The Imperfect Genius of the Actors Studio.* Garden City, New York: Doubleday, 1980.

Agan, Patrick. *The Decline and Fall of the Love Goddess.* Los Angeles: Pinnacle Books, 1979.

Anderson, Janice. *Marilyn Monroe.* London: Hamlyn, 1983.

Anger, Kenneth, *Hollywood Babylon,* London: Arrow, 1986.

Arnold, Eve. *Marilyn Monroe: An Appreciation.* London: Hamish Hamilton, 1987.

Austin, John. *Hollywood's Babylon Women.* New York: S.P.I. Books, 1994.

Badman, Keith. *The Final Years of Marilyn Monroe.* London: Aurum, 201

Banner, Lois. *Marilyn: The Passion and The Paradox.* London: Bloomsbury, 2012.

Barson, Michael. *The Illustrated Who's Who of Hollywood Directors.* New York: Farrar, Straus & Giroux, 1995.

Belmont, George. *Silver Marilyn: Marilyn Monroe and the Camera.* New York: Schirmer Mosel, 2007.

Bigsby, Christopher. *Arthur Miller.* London: Phoenix, 2009.

Bosworth, Patricia. *Montgomery Clift: A Biography.* New York: Limelight, 2001.

Bradshaw, John. *Dreams That Money Can Buy: The Tragic Life of Libby Holman.* New York: William Morrow & Co, 1985.

Brater, Enoch. *Arthur Miller: A Playwright's Life and Works.* London: Thames & Hudson, 2005.

Bret, David. *Clark Gable: Tormented Star.* London, Robson, 2007.

Brill, Lesley. *John Huston's Filmmaking.* Cambridge: Cambridge University Press, 1997.

Brown, Peter, and Patte Barham. *Marilyn: The Last Take.* New York: Penguin, 1992.

Capell, Frank A. *The Strange Death of Marilyn Monroe.* Staten Island, New York: Herald of Freedom, 1964.

Carpozi, George Jr. *Marilyn Monroe: Her Own Story.* New York: Belmost, 1961.

Casillo, Charles. *Marilyn Monroe: The Private Life of a Public Icon.* New York: St. Martin's Press, 2018.

Cawthorne, Nigel. *Sex Lives of the Hollywood Goddesses.* London: Prion, 1997.

Churchwell, Sarah. *The Many Lives of Marilyn Monroe.* (London: Granada), 2004.

Clayton, Marie. *Marilyn Monroe: Unseen Archives.* Bath: Parragon, 2005.

Conover, David. *Finding Marilyn.* New York: Grosset & Dunlap, 1981.

Corrigan, Robert, ed. *Arthur Miller: A Collection of Critical Essays.* Englewood Cliffs, NJ: Prentice Hall, 1969.

Crown, Lawrence. *Marilyn at Twentieth Century-Fox*. London: Comet/Planet, 1987.

Curtis, Tony, with Peter Golenbock. *American Prince: My Autobiography*. London: Virgin, 2008.

- With Mark A. Vieira. *Some Like It Hot: Me, Marilyn and the Movie*. London: Virgin, 2009.

Doll, Susan. *Marilyn: Her Life and Legend*. New York: Beekman House, 1990.

Dougherty, James E. *The Secret Happiness of Marilyn Monroe*. Chicago: Playboy Press, 1976.

Eastman, John. *Retakes: Behind the Scenes of 500 Classic Movies*. New York: Ballantine Books, 1989.

Edwards, Anne. *Vivien Leigh: A Biography*. New York: Simon & Schuster, 1977.

Essoe, Gabe. *The Complete Films of Clark Gable*. New York: Citadel, 1994.

Finlayson, Alex. *Plays*. London: Oberon Books, 1998.

Ford, Selwyn. *The Casting Couch: Making It in Hollywood*. London: Grafton Books, 1990.

Freeman, Lucy. *Why Norma Jean Killed Marilyn Monroe*. Mamaroneck Press. New York: Hastings House, 1992.

Garceau, Jean. *The Biography of Clark Gable*. New York: Little Brown & Co., 1961.

Garfield, David. *A Player's Place: The Story of the Actors Studio*. New York: Macmillan, 1980.

Goode, James. *The Making of The Misfits*. New York: Limelight, 1986.

Gottfried, Martin. *Arthur Miller: A Life*. London: Faber and Faber, 2003.

Grant, Neil, ed. *Clark Gable In His Own Words*. London: Hamlyn, 1992.

Grobel, Lawrence. *The Huston's: The Life and Times of a Hollywood Dynasty*. New York: Skyhorse Publishing, 2014.

Guiles, Fred Lawrence. *Norma Jean: The Life of Marilyn Monroe*. London: Granada, 1985.

*Legend: The Life and Death of Marilyn Monroe*. Lanham, MD: Scarborough House, 1991.

Gussow, Mel. *Conversations with Arthur Miller*. New York: Applause, 2002.

Hadleigh, Boze. *Hollywood Babble On: Stars Gossip About Other Stars*. London: Birch Lane, 1994.

Hamblett, Charles. *Who Killed Marilyn Monroe?* London: Leslie Frewin, 1966.

Harris, Radie. *Radie's New World*. New York: W.H. Allen, 1975.

Haspiel, James. *Marilyn: The Ultimate Look at the Legend*. London: Blake, 2006.

Hoskyns, Barney, *Montgomery Clift: Beautiful Loser*. London: Bloomsbury, 1991.

Hudson, James A. *The Mysterious Death of Marilyn Monroe*. New York: Volitant, 1968.

Huston, John. *An Open Book*. New York: Alfred A. Knopf, 1980.

Jarski, Rosemarie. *Hollywood Wit*. London: Prion, 2000.

Jordan, Ted. *Norma Jean: A Hollywood Love Story*. London: Pan Books, 1990.

Kahn, Roger. *Joe and Marilyn: A Memory of Love*. New York: Morrow, 1986.

Kaminsky, Stuart. *John Huston: Maker of Magic*. Boston: Houghton Mifflin, 1978.

Kanfer, Stefan. *Somebody: The Reckless Life and Remarkable Career of Marlon Brando*. London: Faber and Faber, 2008.

Kidder, Clark. *Marilyn Monroe: Cover to Cover*. Iola, WI: Krause Publications, 1999.

Kobal, John, ed. *Marilyn Monroe: A Life of Film*. London: Hamlyn, 1974.

LaGuardia, Robert. *Monty: A Biography of Montgomery Clift*. New York: Avon, 1977.

Lancaster, David. *Montgomery Clift*. Scarborough, Bath: Absolute Press. 2005.

Lawford, Patricia Seaton, with Ted Schwarz. *Peter Lawford: Mixing with Monroe, the Kennedys, the Rat Pack and the Whole Damn Crowd*. London: Futura, 1990.

Leaming, Barbara. *Marilyn Monroe*. London: Orion, 2002.

Leonard, Maurice. *Montgomery Clift*. London: Hodder & Stoughton, 1997.

Luijters, Guus, ed., *Marilyn Monroe In Her Own Words*. London: Omnibus Press, 1990.

Madsen, Axel. *John Huston*. London: Robson, 1979.

Mailer, Norman. *Of Women and Their Elegance*. New York: Simon & Schuster, 1980.

*Marilyn*. London, Virgin, 2012.

Mann, William J. *The Contender: The Story of Marlon Brando*. New York: HarperCollins, 2019.

Maslon, Laurence. *Some Like It Hot: The Official 50ᵗʰ Anniversary Companion*. London: Pavilion, 2009.

McCann, Graham. *Marilyn Monroe*. New Brunswick, NJ. Rutgers University Press, 1988.

McClelland, Doug, ed., *Hollywood on Hollywood: Tinsel Town Talks*. Winchester, MA: Faber & Faber, 1985.

- *StarSpeak: Hollywood on Everything*. Winchester, MA: Faber & Faber, 1987.

McGilligan, Patrick. *George Cukor: A Double Life*. London: Faber and Faber, 1991.

Mellen, Joan. *Marilyn Monroe*. London: W.H. Allen, 1974.

Meyers, Jeffrey. *The Genius and the Goddess*. London: Arrow, 2010.

Miller, Arthur. *Timebends: A Life*. London: Methuen, 1987.

- *After the Fall*. London: Penguin, 1992.

- *Plays: Six*. London: Methuen, 2009.

- *Presence: Collected Stories of Arthur Miller*. London: Bloomsbury, 2010. and Serge Toubiana.

- *The Misfits: Story of a Shoot*. New York: Phaidon, 2011.

Montand, Yves. *You See, I Haven't Forgotten*. London: Chatto & Windus, 1992.

Morella, Joe, and Edward Z. Epstein. *Rebels: The Rebel Hero in Films*. New York: Citadel Press, 1971.

Morgan, Michelle. *Marilyn Monroe*. London: Constable & Robinson, 2012.

Moss, Leonard. *Arthur Miller*. Boston: Twayne, 1980.

Murray, Eunice. *The Last Months*. New York: Pyramid, 1975.

Nolan, William F. *John Huston: King Rebel*. Los Angeles, CA: Sherbourne Press, 1965.

Osborne, Robert. *80 Years of the Oscar: The Official History of the Academy Awards*. New York: Abbeville, 2008.

Parish, James Robert. *Hollywood Divas: The Good, the Bad and the Fabulous*. New York: Contemporary Books, 2003.

Parker, John. *Five for Hollywood*. New York: Carol Publishing, 1991.

Peary, Danny. *Close-Ups*. New York: Galahad Books, 1978.

Pepitone, Lena and William Stadiem. *Marilyn Monroe Confidential*. New York: Pocket Books, 1980.

Pratley, Gerald. *The Cinema of John Huston*. South Brunswick and New York: A.S. Barnes, 1977.

Riese, Randall, and Neal Hitchens. *The Unabridged Marilyn: Her Life from A to Z*. New York: Random House Value Publishing, 1990.

Roberts, Jerry, ed., *Mitchum In his Own Words*. New York: Limelight, 2000.

Rollyson, Carl E. *Marilyn Monroe: A Life of the Actress*. London: New English Library, 1990.

Rosen, Marjorie. *Popcorn Venus: Women, Movies and the American Dream*. New York: Avon Books, 1973.

Rosten, Norman. *Marilyn: An Untold Story*. New York: Signet, 1973.

Samuels, Charles. *The King of Hollywood: A Biography of Clark Gable*. London: W.H. Allen, 1962.

Schneider, Michel. *Marilyn's Last Sessions*. Edinburgh: Canongate, 2006.

Shipman, David, ed., *Movie Talk: Who Said What About Whom in the Movies*. London: Bloomsbury, 1988.

Signoret, Simone. *Nostalgia Isn't What It Used to Be*. New York: Penguin, 1979.

Skolsky, Sidney. *Marilyn*. New York: Dell, 1954.

Slatzer, Robert F. *The Marilyn Files*. New York: Shapolsky, 1992.

Spada, James. *Peter Lawford: The Man Who Kept the Secrets*. New York: Bantam Books, 1992.

Spoto, Donald. *Laurence Olivier: A Biography*. New York: HarperCollins, 1992.

*Marilyn Monroe: The Biography*. London: Arrow, 1994.

Steinem, Gloria. *Marilyn: Norma Jeane*. New York: Signet, 1988.

Strasberg, Susan. *Marilyn and Me*. London: Bantam, 1993.

Summers, Anthony. *Goddess: The Secret Lives of Marilyn Monroe*. London: Orion, 1985.

Taraborelli, J. Randy. *The Secret Life of Marilyn Monroe*. London: Pan, 2010.

Tosches, Nick. *Dino: Living High in the Dirty Business of Dreams*. London: Minerva, 1993.

Tozzi, Romano. *John Huston: A Picture Treasury of his Films*. New York: Falcon Enterprizes, 1971.

Underwood, Peter. *Death in Hollywood*. London: Piatkus, 1992.

Wallach, Eli. *The Good, the Bad and Me*. Orlando, Fl: Harcourt Inc., 2005.

Wayne. Jane Ellen. *Gable's Women*. New York: Prentice Hall Press, 1987.

*Clark Gable: Portrait of a Misfit*. London: Robson, 1993.

Weatherby, W.J. *Conversations with Marilyn*. London: Sphere, 1976.

Welland, Dennis. *Arthur Miller*. New York: Grove Press, 1961.

Winters, Shelley. *Shelley.* London:
Granada, 1981.

*Shelley II: The Middle of My Century.*
New York: Pocket Books, 1989.

Wolfe, Donald H. *The Assassination of
Marilyn Monroe.* London: Warner,
1999.

Zolotow, Maurice. *Billy Wilder in
Hollywood.* New York: Limelight,
1987.

# The Misfits

## The Film That
## Ended a Marriage

### BY
### AUBREY MALONE

Published in the USA by:
BearManor Media
1317 Edgewater Dr #110
Orlando, FL 32804
www.bearmanormedia.com

Perfect ISBN 978-1-62933-939-9
Case ISBN 978-1-62933-940-5
BearManor Media, Orlando, Florida
Printed in the United States of America
Book design by Robbie Adkins, www.adkinsconsult.com

# Contents

# Acknowledgements

Sincere thanks to Steve Cox, a prolific writer and an incorrigible collector of memorabilia, for the vast store of photographs he has provided for this book. Thanks also to United Artists and MGM Home Entertainment for additional images, and to my publisher Ben Ohmart, my editor Stone Wallace, my typesetter Robbie Adkins and my copy editors Derek and Debbie Savage.

# Introduction

*The Misfits* effectively pulled the curtain down on three careers. It had its origin in a short story written by Arthur Miller. The idea of turning it into a screenplay came about after his then wife Marilyn Monroe had an ectopic pregnancy in 1957. She teetered on the edge of a nervous breakdown as she realized she would never be able to have children. Miller suggested she focus on her acting instead. He offered to expand the role of one of the fringe characters in his screenplay - Roslyn - to facilitate this.[1]

Marriage put the brakes on Miller's career as a playwright. Instead he became Monroe's doctor, her psychiatrist and her pill counter. Apart from *The Misfits*, the screenplay that was supposed to strengthen their relationship instead of threatening it, he had little to show for the hours he spent at his desk. Most of what he wrote ended up in the trash can. What didn't, like his lamentable work as script doctor on *Let's Make Love*, the film Monroe made prior to *The Misfits*, was little more than literary prostitution.

The shoot began as Miller reeled from the knowledge that Monroe had had an affair with her *Let's Make Love* co-star Yves Montand while he was working on the screenplay. The affair put the last nail in the coffin of an already crumbling marriage. They couldn't, however, split before the film ended. It would have been bad publicity for it and Miller had to be on set anyway to do the re-writes director John Huston was demanding. As the hot Nevada sun bore down on them they went through the motions of behaving as man and wife, even to the extent of sharing a hotel suite, but their rows on set told a different story.

The film was completed against all the odds. Monroe struggled with an addiction to pills. Miller tried to act nonchalant as she ripped into him with sarcastic asides. But somehow the film got itself made. It may not have fared as well at the box office as most people working on it expected it to do but posterity has come to see it as an iconic valentine to a world that was already disappearing just as surely as the lifestyle of its three main characters. Their fates were mirrored in many ways by the stars playing them as their bodies and minds fell apart. With the benefit of hindsight it's easy to see how the two main characters are thinly-disguised versions of Miller and Monroe. The "reel" couple stayed together while the "real" one didn't but in many other respects the film was an uncanny alliance of life and art.

*The Misfits* occupies the middle range of John Huston's career. It was his seventeenth of 37 films, made twenty years after his first and 26 before his last.

In the opening credits he presents us with an array of puzzle pieces that don't fit. Already we're being prepared for an assortment of characters floundering in empty space.

Miller's screenplay for the film was an amplification of a story he published in *Esquire* magazine in 1957 under the title "The Mustangs." "Misfits" was rodeo slang for a horse that was too small or weak for riding or farm work.

The story has three main characters: Gaylord, Perce and Guido. All of them have suffered loss in their lives. Gaylord's wife was unfaithful to him. Perce was disinherited from his house after his father died and his mother re-married, Guido's wife died in childbirth.

A fourth character, Roslyn, is Gay's separated wife. She doesn't appear. Miller made her into a central figure in his screenplay, basing her on a character from another one of his stories, "Please Don't Kill Anything," which he wrote years before. Monroe would of course play her in the film. The other two main stars were Clark Gable (Gay) and Montgomery Clift (Perce).

The three men live in the past. They remember times when things were better for them. Gay pines for his wife. Perce goes from rodeo to rodeo trying to take his mind off his restlessness. Guido spends his time trying to renovate the house he lived in with his ill-fated wife but never quite finishes it. The fact that they live in Reno, a transient city where people come to put the seal on dead relationships seems apt. They meet women interested in casual flings, relationships without strings.